AMPHIBIANS & REPTILES
In Alaska, The Yukon & Northwest Territories

AMPHIBIANS & REPTILES
In Alaska, The Yukon & Northwest Territories

ROBERT PARKER HODGE

ALASKA NORTHWEST PUBLISHING COMPANY
Anchorage, Alaska

Copyright © 1976
Robert Parker Hodge

All rights reserved. No part of this book may be reproduced or transmitted in any form or by any means, electronic or mechanical, including photocopying, recording or by any information storage and retrieval system, without written permission of Alaska Northwest Publishing Company.

First printing: June 1976
Second printing: December 1977

Library of Congress cataloging in publication data:
Hodge, Robert Parker, 1938-
    Amphibians and reptiles in Alaska, the Yukon, and Northwest Territories.
    Bibliography: p.
    SUMMARY: A discussion of arctic and subarctic herpetofauna, specifically of northern North America, with a guide to identifying these animals.
    1. Reptiles—Alaska—Identification. 2. Reptiles—Yukon Territory—Identification. 3. Reptiles—Northwest Territories—Identification. 4. Amphibians—Alaska—Identification. 5. Amphibians—Yukon Territory—Identification. 6. Amphibians—Northwest Territories—Identification. [1. Reptiles. 2. Amphibians] I. Title.
QL653.A4H6   598.1'09798   76-8517
ISBN 0-88240-065-7

Alaska Northwest Publishing Company
Box 4-EEE, Anchorage, Alaska 99509
Printed in U.S.A.

Cover—Mating boreal toads, *Bufo boreas*, seen near Juneau, Alaska. The background is a coastal spruce and hemlock forest near Wrangell, Alaska.

For those growing up in the North . . . especially Heather.

CONTENTS

Preface ix

INTRODUCTION 1

AMPHIBIANS AND REPTILES 3
What are amphibians and reptiles? 3
Life history 5
Geographical distribution and origin 12
Northern adaptations 17

MYTHOLOGY, RELIGION
AND SUPERSTITION 25

IN ALASKA 31
Physiography, climate and vegetation of Alaska 31
Check list of species present in Alaska 43
    Rough-skinned newt, northwestern salamander,
    long-toed salamander, boreal toad, spotted
    frog, wood frog.
Other species that may be present in Alaska 57

IN THE YUKON AND
NORTHWEST TERRITORIES 61
Physiography, climate and vegetation of the
Yukon and Northwest Territories 62
James Bay 63
Check list of species present in the Yukon
and Northwest Territories 65
    Canadian toad, Hudson Bay toad, chorus frog,
    wood frog, leopard frog, garter snake.
Other species that may be present in the Yukon
and Northwest Territories 78

WHAT YOU CAN DO 79
Appendix: Herpetological collections of the Tongass
Historical Society Museum, Ketchikan, Alaska 81

Reading list 83

PREFACE

There is very little popular literature available today dealing with *northern* amphibians and reptiles. Bookshelves are filled with bird, mammal and mushroom guides, but those seeking information about northern frogs and snakes are forced to search far and wide for occasional references scattered throughout the literature. This book specifically concerns itself with northern North America (Alaska, Yukon and Northwest Territories) but some effort is made to discuss arctic and subarctic amphibians and reptiles found throughout the world. It is the purpose of this book to provide a concise, nontechnical, although hopefully accurate, interpretive guide for the people of the North. Readers who desire more comprehensive or technical information will find the extensive reading list valuable.

Identifying frogs, toads, salamanders and snakes may seem difficult for individuals not familiar with the animals involved. Unfortunately, traditional identification keys often do little to help. Because Alaska and the Yukon and Northwest Territories have species of amphibians and reptiles that are quite distinct from each other, the photographs in this guide will make the native varieties readily identifiable. Color and pattern vary considerably in individual species, yet certain distinguishing characteristics, which are pointed out in the illustrations, will normally indicate the species involved with little difficulty.

I am grateful to the following for assistance during the preparation of this book:

J. Alquire, W. Berry, J.A. Blackburn, B. Bleckert,
G. Breese, B. Bromfield and the grade 3 class of the Moosonee Ontario school, D. Blankenbeckler, R. Brown,
J. Bryson, C. Cadzow, S. Campbell, W. B. Carey,
M. Carr, C. H. Chapman, K. Clark, B. Copeland, J. Coppess,
J. Gowran, B. DeArnold, D. Day, J. Donohue,
W. Eisenbart, L. Ellenburg, J. Fergeson, R. Finch,
J. B. Fitzgerald, E. Fortier, R. Furness, S. Germaine and the students of Ocean View Elementary School, Anchorage,
R. Goertson, W. J. Graves, T. Grenshaw, F. J. Vonder Haar,
M. Hursh, E. Kalkine, R. Keep, W. A. Kenyon, M. Knight,

A. Lamb, R. Lance, C. Lane, P. Edgell, Fort Vermilion School, Alberta, B. Maahs, H. Markan, C. Maser, L. Marx, V. McGillvray, W. Meehan, M. Messersmith, J. Massin, G. Meudal, J. D. Miller, R. Miller, the Monus family, C. Moore, R. Nelson, T. Nichols, E. R. Norman, E. E. Oliver, N. Panter, Pelican School children, G. Pendlebury, R. Prasil, S. Prunella, B. Rinehart, J. Rawle, L. J. Rowinski, T. Saunders, J. Scott, D. Sellards, B. Sheridan, F. Slavens, H. E. Stanley, P. Smith, T. Smith, the Schwarze family, Vancouver Public Aquarium, S. L. Stewart, B. Thomas, M. A. Voss, W. Ulmer, H. Waldron, F. Wigg Jr., Alaska Department of Fish & Game, E. Whitesel.

The American Geographical Society gave me permission to base several maps on maps that appeared in "Geography of the Northlands."

The following are quoted with permission from sources stated: *The Twelve Seasons,* Joseph Wood Krutch, Investment Dealer's Digest. *The Coming of the Pond Fishes,* Ben Hur Lampman (Caroline Lampman Cooper), Binfort & Mort Publishers. *Reptiles and Amphibians in Massachusetts,* J. D. Lazell, Massachusetts Audubon Society. *Runes of the North,* Sigurd F. Olson, Alfred A. Knopf, Inc. *Tales from the Longhouse,* Gray's Publishing Ltd.

For criticism of the manuscript, I am indebted to Dr. James Morrow, Department of Biology, University of Alaska, and Robert Maahs, Former Secretary and Editor, Southwestern Herpetological Society. Special thanks to my wife, and to my mother, who typed the manuscript.

I have often wondered that a world which pretends to mark so many days and to celebrate so many occasions should accept quite so casually the day when Hyla crucifer *(spring peeper) announces that winter is over. One swallow does not make a spring, and the robin arrives with all the philistine unconcern of a worldling back from his Winter at Aiken or Palm Beach. But the peeper seems to realize, rather better than we, the significance of his resurrection, and I wonder if there is any other phenomenon in the heavens above or in the earth beneath which so simply and so definitely announces that life is resurgent again.*

Joseph Wood Krutch
THE TWELVE SEASONS

INTRODUCTION

Herpetology is the science that deals with amphibians and reptiles. The word comes from the Greek *HERPETON* (a creeping thing) and concerns two groups of animals, the amphibians (frogs, toads, salamanders, caecilians) and reptiles (crocodiles, turtles, snakes, lizards, tuatara). Living representatives of these little understood and often maligned groups of animals are found on every continent except Antarctica. Representatives of both groups are found well above the Arctic Circle in the Northern Hemisphere and south of the equator to the tips of South America, Tasmania, New Zealand and South Africa.

Situated as they are geographically, Alaska and the Canadian territories have a somewhat impoverished herpetofauna when compared with areas closer to the equator. However, the hardy amphibians and reptiles that reside in northern regions are often locally abundant and offer residents of these areas the opportunity to observe and familiarize themselves with a little known aspect of northern life.

The published history of the herpetology of Alaska and the Canadian territories is scant and incomplete. Nothing has been assembled which treats this region's herpetofauna as a whole. The first references to Alaskan amphibians and reptiles appeared in the late 1800's when explorers sent representative specimens to the large eastern museums. In 1882 three worm salamanders turned up in the Smithsonian Institution, their point of origin listed as Hassler Harbor (Annette Island) and Yakutat, and created a herpetological enigma that remains unsolved to this day. These salamanders, *Batrachoseps caudatus* (*Batrachoseps* refers to the frog or toadlike head and *caudatus* means having a tail), were first described in 1889 from specimens sent to the Smithsonian by a Captain Nichols, United States Navy, commander of the survey steamer *Hassler,* which made extensive surveys in Southeastern Alaska between 1881 and 1883. Nichols was at Hassler Harbor on August 10, 1882. While in Southeastern Alaska, Nichols shipped numerous specimens to the Smithsonian and earned a respected reputation as a collector.

Other worm salamanders are found in Oregon, California and Mexico but for over 75 years no additional specimens have been found in Alaska, leading many scientists to question the authenticity of the locality data. Most contemporary biologists place little credence on *Batrachoseps caudatus*—either the locality record or the species. They do acknowledge, however, that little collecting has been done in Alaska and that present distribution of the genus *Batrachoseps* suggests a once far ranging group of primitive salamanders (there is another questionable isolated *Batrachoseps* record from central Mexico), now restricted to a few isolated specialized environments.

While the exact status of the Alaska worm salamander remains in doubt, Alaska can unquestionably lay claim to six other species of amphibians presently residing within her boundaries. One species of reptile, the garter snake, has occasionally been sighted and in one instance was captured in Alaska, but it remains to be established whether snakes are in fact residents of the state. Garter snakes are, however, common in the Northwest Territories, as are five species of amphibians. Only one species of amphibian is known from the Yukon.

AMPHIBIANS & REPTILES

"They may not sing as well or prettily as the birds, but, as others before me have pointed out, the frogs did it first."

       James D. Lazell Jr.
       REPTILES & AMPHIBIANS IN
       MASSACHUSETTS

WHAT ARE AMPHIBIANS AND REPTILES?

Amphibians and reptiles are ectotherms (their body temperature is largely dependent on external forces) located evolutionarily between the fishes and the higher vertebrates (birds and mammals). Abundant in tropical and temperate regions of the world, their numbers decrease as latitude increases. All amphibians and reptiles now living in Alaska and the Canadian territories reach the northern limits of their distribution within the boundaries of the state and territories. Most are widely distributed in more southern latitudes of North America.

Amphibians (frogs, toads, salamanders and the wormlike tropical caecilians) are moist-skinned, scaleless animals without claws. The skin is smooth or warty and is usually supplied with mucous and granular glands, the latter secreting a toxic substance harmful to small predatory animals. Most species have lungs; a few depend entirely on their moist skin for respiration. All are dependent on moisture for survival. The majority lay their naked eggs (protected only by a jelly envelope) in water; the young go through an aquatic larval stage and eventually metamorphose into adults. A few, such as worm salamanders, are completely terrestrial; the eggs are deposited in moist situations under fallen logs where the gilled larval stage is passed inside the

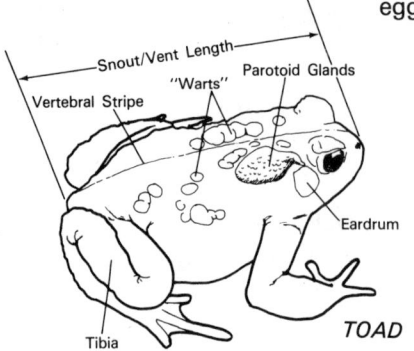

TOAD

egg before hatching. Most amphibians are secretive, spending the daylight hours under logs, boards, rocks and other ground debris. Salamanders are generally considered to be voiceless, but frogs and toads (primarily males) can produce sound.

Reptiles (lizards, snakes, crocodiles, turtles and the evolutionary relict, tuatara) have a hard dry body covering of scales or plates, and well-developed claws on the feet. They breathe with lungs, and the majority lay a leathery-shelled "land egg." A few are viviparous—that is, they produce living young rather than eggs.

Reptiles do not have an independent aquatic larval stage; they are born or hatched from eggs as miniature replicas of their parents. The majority are diurnal, active during the daylight hours; and they are generally more dependent on warmth and sunshine than are the amphibians.

SALAMANDER

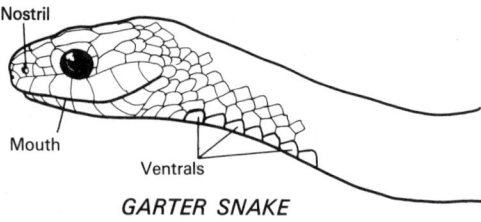

GARTER SNAKE

LIFE HISTORY

All amphibians of Alaska and the Canadian territories (with the exception of the enigmatic *Batrachoseps caudatus*) share a similar life history. The cold winter months are spent in hibernation. With the advent of spring warmth, the adults awaken and migrate to the breeding ponds. Salamanders are commonly seen abroad at this time and the air is filled with the vocalizations of frogs and toads. Mating and egg deposition take place in the water.

Female frogs are attracted to the males by their vocalizations. The smaller male embraces the larger female from above. Fertilization is external: the female releases the eggs directly into the water, whereupon the male floods them with sperm. The voiceless salamanders recognize their mates by smell. Elaborate courtship dances follow in which the male induces the female to pick up the spermatophore (a small jelly-covered package containing the sperm), which he has deposited on the pond bottom, with her cloaca. The eggs are thereby fertilized internally.

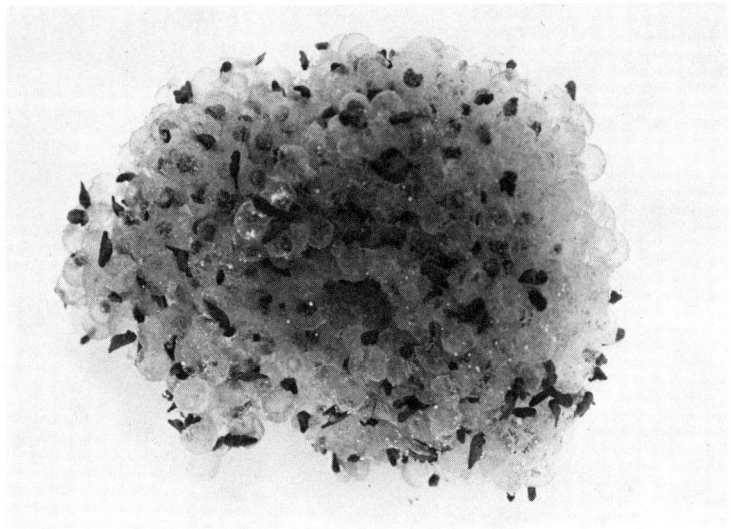

Wood frog egg mass from Anchorage, Alaska. Numerous tadpoles can be seen hatching on the outer margins.

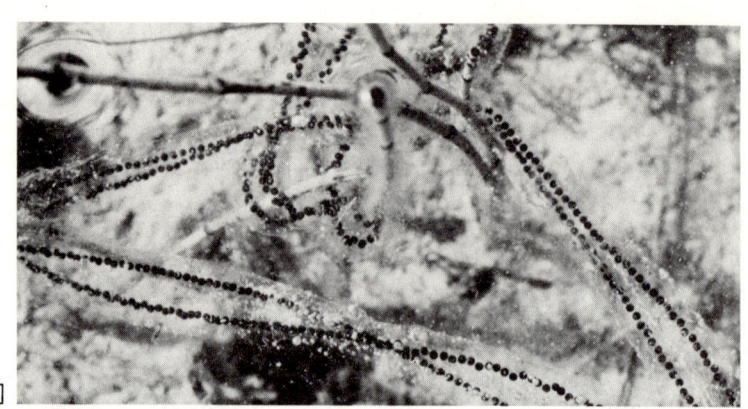

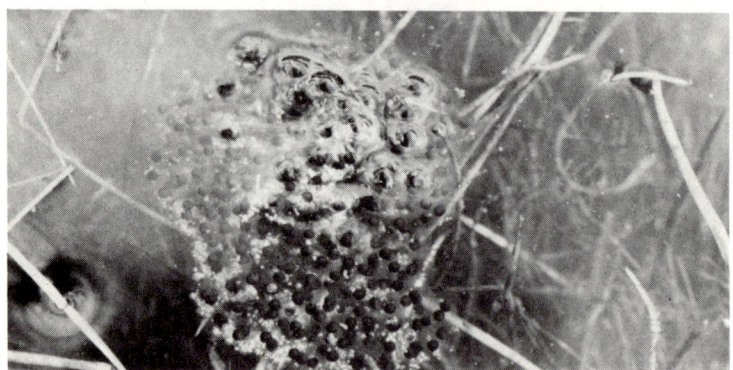

[1] *Boreal toad eggs near Yakutat.* [2] *Several wood frog egg masses near Fairbanks.* [3] *Individual wood frog egg mass.*

Newt

Singly, attached to vegetation

Long-Toed Salamander

Small clusters, attached to vegetation

Northwestern Salamander
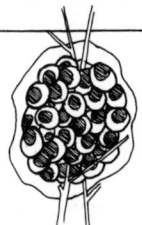
Large firm clusters, attached to sticks

Toad
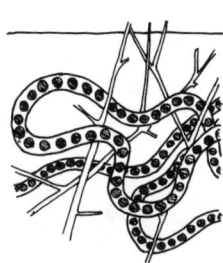
Tangled strings

Spotted Frog
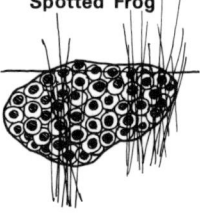
Close to shore, floating, often unattached

Wood Frog
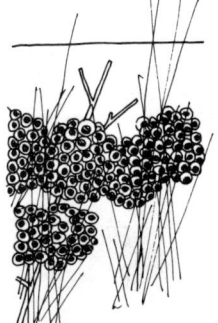
Beneath the surface, attached to vegetation in numerous small clumps

Alaskan amphibian egg masses (not to scale).

Amphibian eggs develop rapidly and hatch into aquatic salamander larvae and frog and toad tadpoles. Metamorphosis, the process whereby the larvae and tadpoles transform from aquatic gill-breathing juveniles into terrestrial lung-breathing adults, usually takes place at the end of the first summer.

Some frogs and salamanders fail to metamorphose during their natal year and retain larval characteristics for extended periods of time, a process called neoteny. Neoteny is rare in frogs (*Rana*) but common in various groups of salamanders (*Ambystoma, Dicamptodon*); and a number of North American forms occasionally reach sexual maturity in the aquatic or larval stage and remain permanent larvae. Several ponds investigated in the

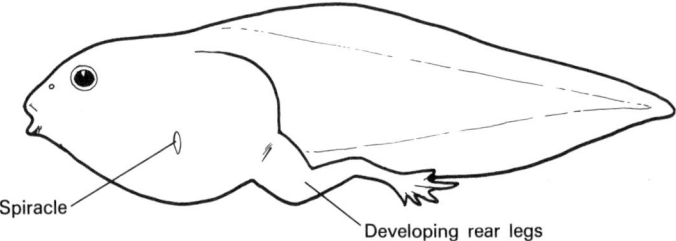

TOAD tadpole is uniformly black. To 1 ½ inches. WOOD FROG tadpole has green-brown body, cream belly, pointed tail tip. Dorsal tail fin terminates at spiracle (small opening to outside from gill chamber). To 2 inches. SPOTTED FROG tadpole has long tail with small flecks and blotches. Dorsal tail fin terminates posterior to spiracle.

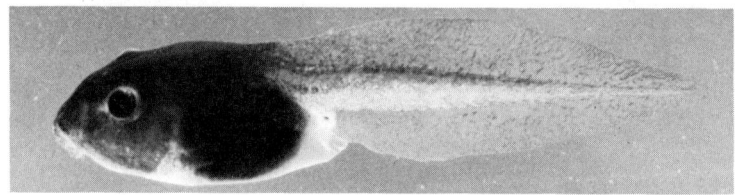

Wood frog tadpole from Anchorage, Alaska.

Wrangell and Ketchikan areas, ponds that do not freeze solid during the winter, contained larval rough-skinned newts of two different age groups, indicating a 2-year metamorphosis cycle. Small larvae from these ponds kept in the laboratory required 2 years to complete metamorphosis. It is not known whether northwestern and long-toed salamanders are occasionally neotenic in Alaska, but neoteny is common in populations of northwestern salamanders from Kitimat, British Columbia, just south of the Alaska border.

The thyroid gland plays a major role in metamorphosis. It is generally believed that when a salamander is neotenic its thyroid does not function properly or the tissues that normally respond to

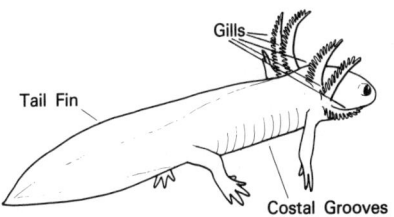

NORTHWESTERN SALAMANDER larva has roughened strip at juncture of tail fin with tail musculature, similar zone in parotid regions. Mottled light and dark green-brown. To 3 ½ inches. NEWT larva has body with two or more rows of light spots forming a light longitudinal stripe. To 2 ½ inches. LONG-TOED SALAMANDER larva uniformly light greenish gray, flecked and mottled with dark brown and black. To 2 inches.

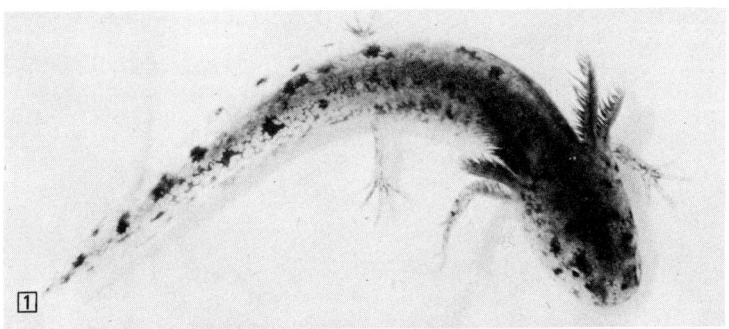

1 Larva and 2 neotenic preserved specimen of northwestern salamander from British Columbia. The latter preserved specimen was collected near Kitimat.

the thyroid have reduced sensitivity to it. Several environmental factors are believed to play an important part in thyroid function, and therefore in neoteny, including temperature extremes (cold), altitude, the acidity-alkalinity of the water as well as its depth, time of egg deposition, availability of food, density of population and amount of iodine in the water. Mountain stream-dwelling salamanders (*Dicamptodon*) in other areas of the United States are commonly neotenic, indicating the apparent influence of cold and high altitude on inhibiting or prolonging metamorphosis. Apparently, in Southeastern Alaska, where similar conditions exist—the summers are relatively cool and short, and where egg deposition often does not commence until summer, salamanders that in the southern parts of their range commonly metamorphose during their natal year require 2 years to complete metamorphosis.

Adult frogs, toads and newts are active during daylight hours when they search for insects and other small animals for food. Other salamanders are nocturnal and quite secretive, hiding under surface litter in moist areas. With the approach of freezing weather, Alaskan amphibians retreat to suitable places for hibernation.

Shed garter snake skin from Northwest Territories.

Northern reptiles, like amphibians, hibernate during the winter months. Snakes often congregate in considerable numbers in dens located in deep fissures in rock outcroppings, below the frost line. Snakes are active during the day, when they search for insects, worms and amphibians for food. Mating takes place on land and females of northern species give birth to fully developed young, which are miniature replicas of their parents. Periodically, snakes shed their outgrown skin. The complete skin, including the covering of the eyes, is sloughed in a smooth operation. The skin is worked loose around the nose by rubbing against abrasive objects and then simply turned inside out as the snake crawls out of its old skin.

The enemies of amphibians and reptiles are many. They are preyed upon by all vertebrates, including other amphibians and reptiles, fish, birds and mammals. Predaceous invertebrates such as beetles, hydra and aquatic insect larvae prey upon tadpoles. Few amphibians and reptiles die of old age. Man, directly and indirectly, via agricultural poisons, insecticides, land reclamation and urban development, takes an increasing toll of amphibians and reptiles.

Seagull predation on boreal toads near Ketchikan, Alaska. The bodies of eviscerated toads litter the pond margins during the breeding season.

GEOGRAPHICAL DISTRIBUTION AND ORIGIN

In studying the geographical distribution and origin of northern amphibians and reptiles, certain relevant facts concerning the earth's history, and more specifically the part Alaska played in that history, must be taken into consideration.

Today water covers about 71% of the earth's surface and existing land masses are not distributed uniformly. Present-day continents, with the exception of Antarctica, are separated by shallow water studded with islands, which, as a result of changes in sea level, have at various times in the past functioned as land bridges between the major continents. The continents themselves have changed their positions significantly, evidence indicating that all present continents were once part of a large unified land mass. During the Cretaceous period, this mass broke up and drifted into a form, roughly approximate to the earth today, typified by large amounts of interconnected land north of the equator and, south of the equator, small land masses widely separated from one another by oceans. The surface features of the continents themselves have been dynamically unstable, with earthquakes, fault movements, and volcanic activity creating the diverse topography evident today. Significant from a zoogeographical standpoint are the extensive mountain ranges, many of which form north-south corridors which restrict longitudinal dispersal while encouraging latitudinal dispersal.

The climate and the resulting vegetation likewise have changed drastically through the ages. As late as the early Tertiary period there was little temperature variation due to latitude, and the Pacific Rim supported a warm humid climate with a resulting forest extending from Japan through Siberia, Beringia, Alaska and south into Oregon. Up to mid-Tertiary, plant and animal communities of Eurasia and North America were almost identical. Turtles and alligators were found in these northern forests far north of their present limits of distribution. In the mid- to late Miocene a severe decline in summer temperatures resulted in the breakup of this humid forest. Along with this cooling trend, the submergence of the Bering land bridge isolated the flora and fauna of North America and Eurasia. The Bering land bridge was again exposed at various times during the Tertiary, but the climate was now boreal and the flora and fauna of Asia and North

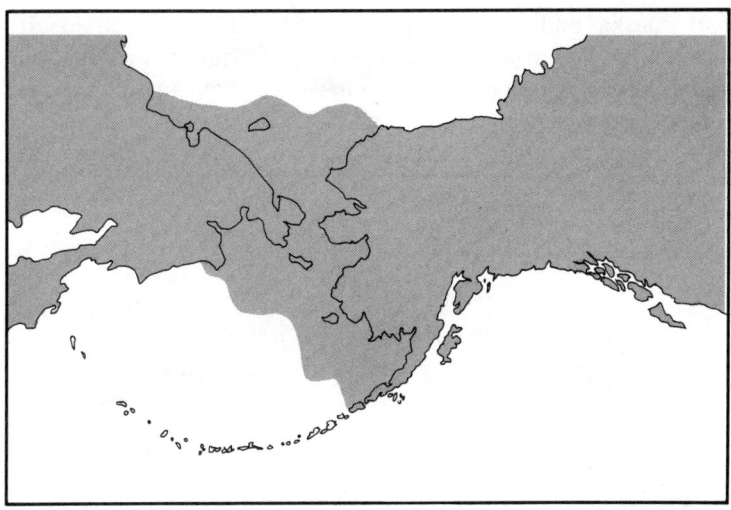

One million years ago the Bering Land Bridge served as a highway for the intercontinental migrations of animals.

America were different, consisting of separate, although similar, northern forest and forest-tundra, and cold-adapted animals.

Factors that affect the dispersal of amphibians and reptiles are many. Generally, amphibians are more tolerant of cold and more dependent on moisture than reptiles. Reptiles, more tolerant of aridity and dependent on warmth, also are much more tolerant of salt water. We generally find a greater diversity of amphibians in cool moist areas and a greater diversity of reptiles in warm dry areas and on oceanic islands. Both amphibians and reptiles are found north of the Arctic Circle and to the southern tips of the land masses in the Southern Hemisphere.

Living amphibians and reptiles are relicts of ancient and dominant groups of animals that are largely extinct today. The first amphibians probably arose during the Devonian period and the first reptiles during the Carboniferous. Reptiles dominated the scene until the advent of the birds and mammals. Today, we have but a minute representation of once widespread and diverse groups of animals.

The present dispersal of most living amphibians and reptiles probably occurred during relatively recent times, long after the continents were in the approximate position they are today. The part Alaska and the Bering land bridge have played in the intercontinental migrations of animals, particularly mammals, is widely known. Other groups of animals, including amphibians and reptiles, have also migrated over Beringia at various times.

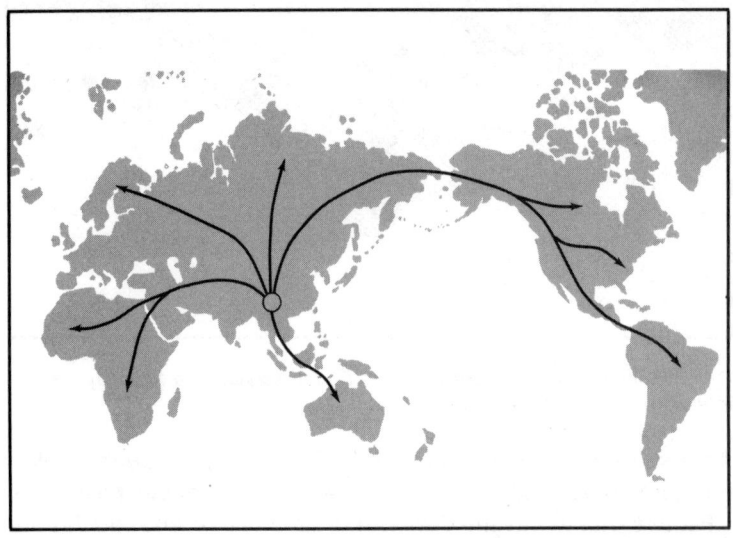

After arising in the tropics of Southeast Asia, frogs of the genus Rana *apparently reached North and South America via the Bering Land Bridge.*

The present distribution of several groups of living amphibians and reptiles illustrates dispersal and extinction over wide areas. Isolated populations of the North American frog *Ascaphus* and the New Zealand *Liopelma,* and of the giant salamanders of southeast Asia and southeast North America, as well as the Pacific Rim affinities of several salamanders, indicate the importance of bridges such as Beringia. Widespread relict populations indicate a past period of dispersal and extinction over northern areas, resulting from changes in climate and vegetation throughout the world.

How groups of amphibians and reptiles passed through the North during their dispersal is well illustrated by the North American wood frog and the Eurasian common frog, two very similar frogs once considered to be one species. Different species of frogs have different development rates, restricting their movement northward. Today only the wood frog and the common frog have the necessary adaptation (a shortened larval period) that allows them to live in the Far North. An ancestral frog of this group evidently crossed the Bering land bridge sometime during the Tertiary period and thereby reached North America, after originating in the Old World tropics and gradually dispersing northward until it was able to make the crossing. Many other amphibians and reptiles have also passed through the same cycle; they arose in the Old or New World tropics and gradually colonized northward until a dominant adaptable species, usually of a large dominant group, made the necessary adaptations to make the crossing.

During the Pleistocene period, mammoth glaciers advanced over vast areas of the Northern Hemisphere, forcing animals and plants to seek refuge south of the glacier margins or in isolated pockets of ice-free areas inside the glacial area. Apparently, four or five major glacial advances covered vast areas of North America. However, during the last glaciation, large areas of Alaska and extreme western Yukon Territory remained ice free, supporting a rich tundra vegetation with isolated pockets of forested country, such as that on the Seward Peninsula and in the area of the present Yukon River Delta. These forested areas served as refuges for many boreal animals.

Exactly where amphibians and reptiles now living in Alaska and the Canadian territories survived glaciation is not positively known, although evidence indicates probable patterns. We can assume that the boreal toad, spotted frog, northwestern salamander, long-toed salamander and newt survived glaciation in the Pacific Refuge and subsequently dispersed northward along the coast and intermontane corridors. It is now believed that many boreal species, such as the chorus frog, leopard frog, Canadian toad and garter snake, survived glaciation in a broad belt of boreal forest south of the glacier and then moved northward, following closely behind the retreat of the glacier. The wood frog, a widely distributed boreal species, likewise survived glaciation in widely scattered areas south of the glacier margins, and it is interesting to speculate if this frog, like many insects and fish, found shelter in the Bering Refuge and subsequently moved eastward and southward where it met wood frogs moving north from refuges south of the glacier margins.

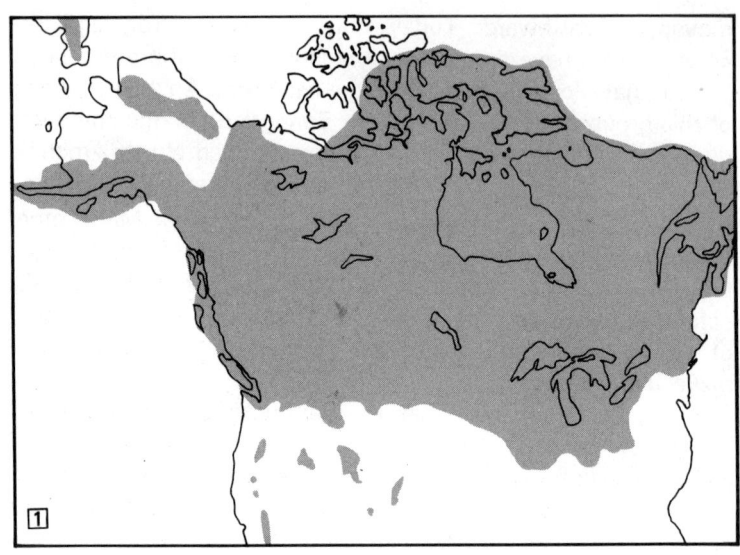

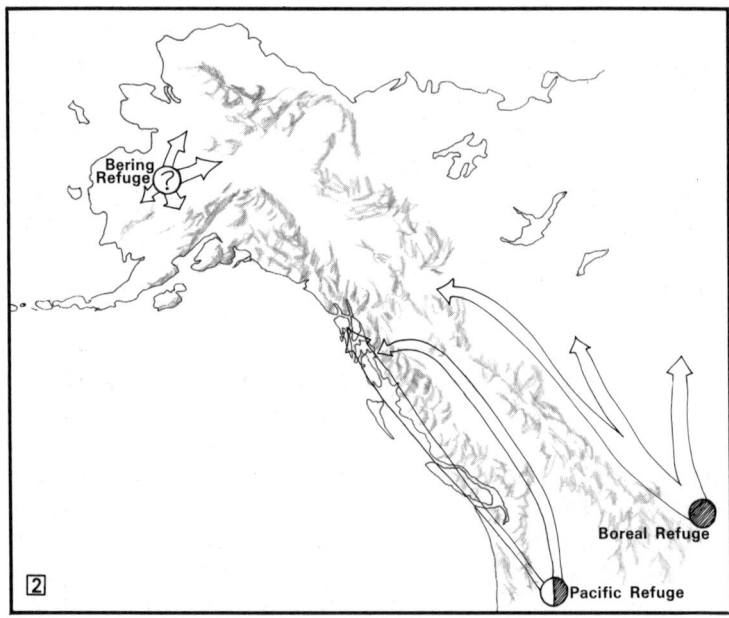

1 During Pleistocene glaciation, much of Alaska and extreme western Yukon Territory were free of ice. 2 After glacial ice receded, amphibians dispersed from refuges along valley routes.

NORTHERN ADAPTATIONS

The precise factors which limit the northern distribution of amphibians and reptiles today are not positively known. However, if we examine the circumpolar distribution of amphibians and reptiles in arctic and subarctic regions of the world, several factors, including temperature, length of summer and availability of suitable places for hibernation, appear to be significant.

Amphibians and reptiles, because their body temperature is dependent on forces outside the body, cannot be considered successful northern colonizers. In the arctic and subarctic, the northern limit of each species may be the latitude at which the larvae of amphibians or embryos of reptiles fail to complete their development in one summer. Several species of salamanders do overwinter as larvae in temperate Southeastern Alaska. However, the shallow ponds which amphibians of the Far North utilize for reproduction freeze solid during the winter, and it is therefore imperative that metamorphosis is completed during the natal summer prior to autumn freezeup. While a certain viviparous Scandinavian reptile commonly requires 2 years for embryonic development, it is not presently known if the viviparous North American garter snake exhibits similar modifications at the northern extremities of its range.

The northward distribution of amphibians coincides rather closely with those areas which have a span of 100 days without

	Mexico	Washington State	Alaska
Frogs/Toads	161	11	3
Salamanders	64	12	3
Turtles	22	4	0
Crocodiles	3	0	0
Snakes	163	10	1(?)
Lizards	112	6	0

killing frosts. Apparently, the length of the summer is critical: it must be warm enough long enough for deposition of eggs, larval development, and metamorphosis.

It is the lack of summer warmth, not the severe cold of winter, that is critical—as long as suitable places for hibernation are available. Wood frogs in the Fairbanks area hibernate in terrestrial situations in shallow (approximately 1.4 inches, or 3.5 centimeters, deep) bowl-shaped pockets or depressions excavated by the frogs in the upper layer of the previous year's dead vegetation. Each

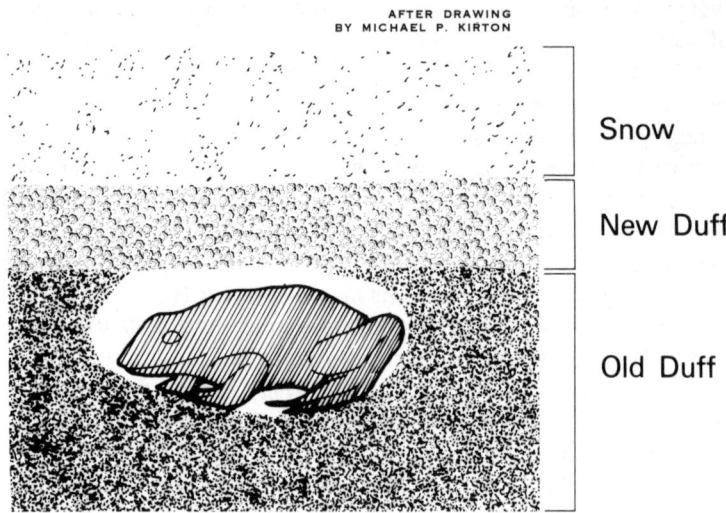

AFTER DRAWING
BY MICHAEL P. KIRTON

Snow

New Duff

Old Duff

pocket is overlaid by an insulating layer of new vegetation which ranges in thickness from 0.6 to 1 inch (1.5 to 2.5 centimeters). Another layer of insulation is provided by snow cover; the deeper the snow, the better the insulation. Years of light snow cover are likely to result in high overwinter mortality.

Such pockets are usually located near water; however, overwintering survival apparently is correlated with the dryness of the actual hibernation site. Mortality apparently is high in moist hibernation sites.

Compared with temperate individuals of the same species, arctic and subarctic wood frogs exhibit a considerably higher weight-length ratio. Energy is used during hibernation—as shown by a decrease in weight over the winter in monitored hibernating frogs. Weight reserves which are evident in northern wood frogs may supply energy reserves for overwintering metabolic needs and, possibly, may serve as insulation against freezing in areas where hibernation may extend to as long as 7 months.

Hibernating wood frogs in the Fairbanks area have been shown to experience temperatures down to 21° F (-6° C) and still survive. It is believed that some type of physiological supercooling must occur, although little is known about this aspect of amphibian hibernation.

Permafrost appears to restrict northward dispersal of many amphibians and reptiles—especially reptiles, the garter snake just reaching the area of sporadic permafrost. In arctic Scandinavia, where two reptiles are common, permafrost is found only in the extreme northern portions. Three amphibians—North American wood frog, Eurasion common frog and Siberian salamander—are found well north into areas of permafrost.

Tundra has long been considered a limiting factor in amphibian and reptile distribution in the Far North. However, the wood frog has recently been recorded in areas considerably north and west of tree line, indicating survival in true tundra conditions.

The known adaptations exhibited by amphibians and reptiles living in northern regions are many. Amphibians which are nocturnal in the more temperate regions of their range exhibit a marked tendency toward diurnal activity in the North, where long hours of daylight are the rule. Wood frogs, which are widely distributed throughout northern and eastern North America, are active during the late evening and early morning hours in the latitude of Minnesota. At Fort Yukon, Alaska, just north of the Arctic Circle, however, activity is concentrated in the warmest and brightest part of the day.

The wood frog has the highest rate of larval development at any given temperature of any North American frog. It is the first to breed in the spring, and the development from egg to tadpole to frog is rapid. It also has the lowest temperature coefficient, indicating that temperature changes have the least effect in modifying the rate of larval development. Finally, eggs, larvae and adults can tolerate lower minimum temperatures than other species.

Other known adaptations of northern amphibians include a marked tendency to submerged egg masses, avoiding the severe temperature fluctuations associated with surface water and increasing chances of survival in case of surface refreezing of the natal pond. The unprotected eggs of amphibians appear to be the most vulnerable stage of development in northern regions. Daytime temperatures might be such that adult frogs could feed and breed at the pond surface and escape to the relatively mild temperatures of the pond bottom with the advent of rapid evening cooling. The eggs, however, could not tolerate the low, often freezing nocturnal temperatures at the surface and would be destroyed. The eggs themselves tend to be larger and darker than those of southern relatives, increasing absorption of radiant energy.

Northern forms of amphibians tend to be considerably smaller than their southern counterparts. Small body size is advantageous in cold regions because it permits rapid exchange of heat between an ectothermic animal and its environment. The animal quickly becomes inactive with the onset of cold weather and promptly becomes active with the resumption of warm weather.

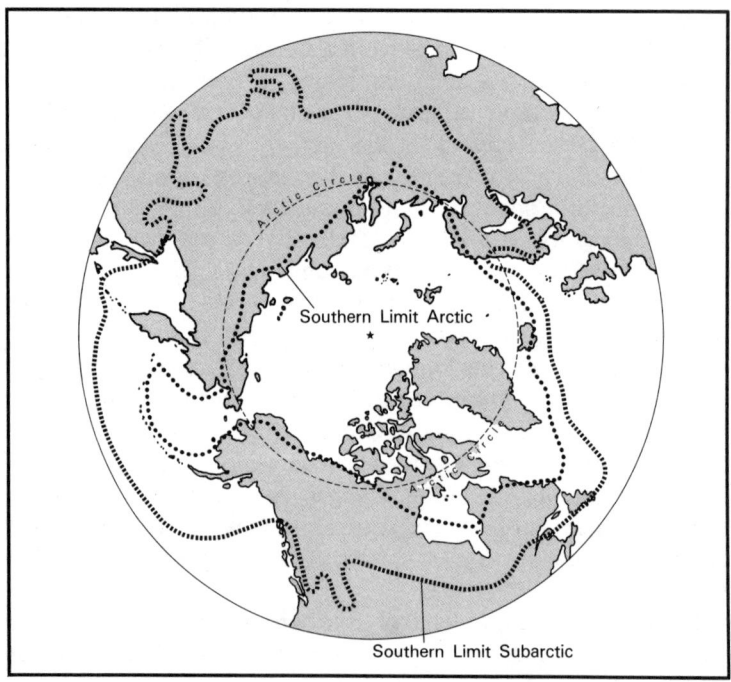

Limits of arctic and subarctic regions.

As a species of frog or toad approaches the higher latitudes, there is a marked tendency toward shortening of the legs. The precise significance of this is not known, but it is believed to reduce the loss of heat and moisture and lessen the chance of freezing—advantages in regions of low temperature and humidity. Shortness of legs may also be associated with burrowing and the decreased activity of the animal due to the short season and lower temperatures.

Many species of animals living in arctic regions exhibit considerable variation in color pattern. Wood frogs from southern

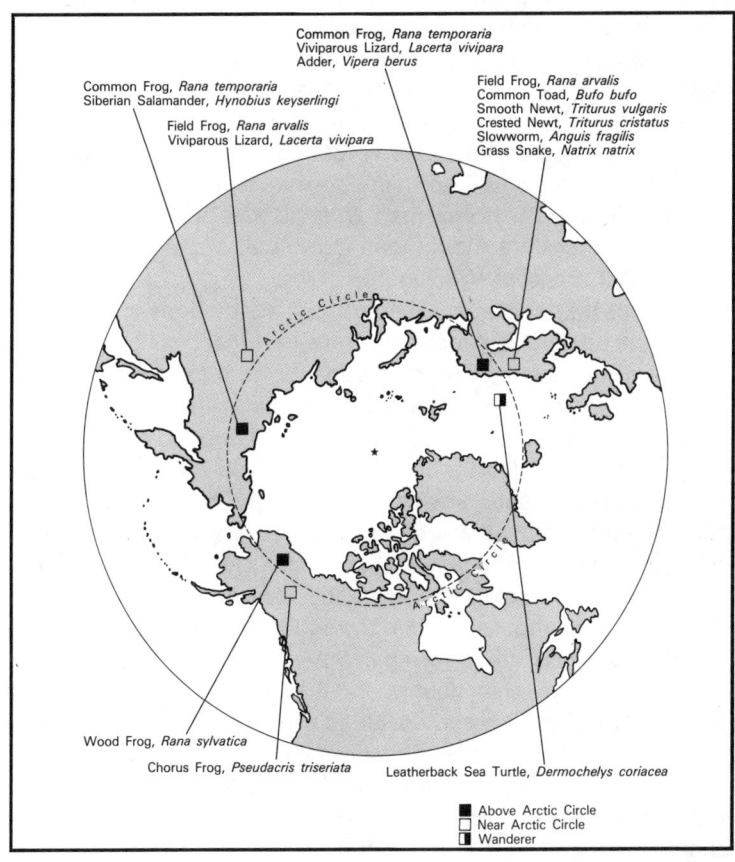

Circumpolar distribution of amphibians and reptiles in the northern hemisphere.

areas of Alaska and most of temperate North America tend to be less conspicuously marked and are more uniformly similar in coloration than frogs from northern Alaska and the Northwest Territories, where there is much variation, even in individual populations. The more conspicuous markings, such as intense middorsal stripe and dark and variable dorsal markings, are conspicuously developed in populations of far northern frogs. This vivid dark coloration might be important to heat economy, dark colors absorb more heat from the sun's energy. Furthermore, this disruptive coloration adds additional protection from predators which is significant in areas of daytime activity.

Generally, amphibians breed earlier in southern areas and progressively later as they approach the northern limits of their distribution. Wood frogs from southeastern United States breed in January, those in Minnesota in early March, and those in northern Alaska in June. However, certain species appear to reverse this process, northern forms breeding earlier than southern forms. The boreal toad, *Bufo boreas,* breeds at an earlier date in Southeastern Alaska than individuals of the same species in sea level areas of Washington state.

Very little is known about the northern adaptations of the garter snake, the one North American reptile that reaches the subarctic. However, the adaptations of the two reptiles that venture into the European arctic are well known. Both are viviparous—as is the North American garter snake—and this is a decided advantage to a reptile in the Far North, because the female is able to incubate the developing young inside her body by moving about and basking for hours in the arctic sun until the young are ready to emerge. A reptile egg would have little chance for success if deposited in the cold earth of arctic regions. It has also been shown that the adder, which in the southern portions of its range breeds and gives birth to young every year, requires 2 years for full development of the young in the northern regions. The developing embryos spend the arctic winter inside the hibernating mother's body. A similar situation is suspected in the garter snake. Northern reptiles show modifications for obtaining heat rather than withstanding cold, again indicating it is the length of summer warmth that is most critical.

If we look at the worldwide northern distribution of amphibians and reptiles, we discover that they extend farthest north in regions where the summers are the longest and the warmest. Some of these areas, particularly in Siberia and central Canada, are also the coldest areas in the world, again indicating that severe winter temperatures are not limiting.

As might be expected, arctic Scandinavia, which has a relatively mild climate due to the moderate maritime conditions which influence it, has the most diverse northern herpetofauna. The common frog, the viviparous lizard, and the poisonous adder all extend well above the Arctic Circle. Six additional species nearly reach the circle and the mild Gulf Stream occasionally carries large tropical marine leatherback turtles to the coast off Norway well above the Arctic Circle. Northern Asia, being somewhat more continental in its influences, has a considerably more impoverished herpetofauna. No Asian reptiles and only two amphibians, the common frog and Siberian salamander, venture above the Arctic Circle. Two others approach the circle in Asia, but fail to reach it. North America fares even worse, only the wood frog being found north of the circle. The minute chorus frog is the only other North American amphibian or reptile that even comes close to the circle. There are no amphibians or reptiles living on the Canadian arctic islands, Greenland or Iceland.

Outside of Scandinavia, with its relatively moderate climate, it is significant that amphibians and reptiles are found farthest north in Asia and North America where the major northward-flowing rivers (Lena, Ob, Yenisei and Yana in Asia and Mackenzie in North America) bring a somewhat moderate influence from more southern areas into arctic regions.

There are no uniquely subarctic or arctic amphibians and reptiles; the northernmost ones belong to dominant groups centered in tropical and temperate areas rather than to cold-adapted groups. The northernmost frogs belong to the widespread dominant tropical and temperate genus *Rana*. The Siberian salamander likewise belongs to a large temperate group of salamanders. Both the reptiles *Lacerta* and *Vipera* are northern representatives of groups widely distributed in the tropics. These northern amphibians and reptiles, which are not that much different from their tropical and temperate relatives, have made the relatively minor adaptations—accelerated larval development in amphibians and viviparity in reptiles—necessary for survival under subarctic and arctic conditions.

ROD BROWN

This contemporary gravestone from Wrangell, Alaska, is interesting because it is obviously a frog rather than the traditional toad.

MYTHOLOGY, RELIGION & SUPERSTITION

The same life flowed in Rana as in me.

Sigurd F. Olson
RUNES OF THE NORTH

The Native people of Alaska, like people everywhere, have legends and stories dealing with amphibians and reptiles. Crests of Frog and Lizard are evident in totemic art throughout Southeastern Alaska, the Totem of the Three Frogs at Wrangell being one of the better known. The frog and lizard of the totem carver and anthropologist are actually toad and salamander. What is obvious to the herpetologist apparently was overlooked by the early anthropologists. The squat, short-legged, fat bodies of the totemic representatives carved in cedar are obviously toadlike, as opposed to the streamlined long-legged form of a frog.

What perhaps is more significant to the herpetologist is the fact that toads are widely distributed throughout totemland and are usually abundant wherever found; they are commonly observed hopping about the backyards of human population centers. Frogs, on the other hand, have a limited distribution in Southeastern Alaska. Similarly, there are no lizards found anywhere in the state, while the salamander is abundant throughout Southeastern Alaska.

To the Native people of Alaska, Frog was guardian spirit, bringer of good fortune, embodiment of wisdom, guide through treacherous country and symbol of secret societies. Its presence endowed its possessor with singing power. Frog plays a significant part in the early religions of Southeastern Alaska; in the beginning Frog and Raven were supernatural companions. Interior Indian and Eskimo mythology is also rich in reference to Frog. Its medicinal values, exaggerated poisonous qualities, and association with bad weather all are evident.

Present-day northern North American amphibians and reptiles have little significance for most human beings. None is poisonous, nor do they have economic or gastronomic importance. Amphibians, frogs and toads in particular, consume enormous quantities of insects during the course of their lives, so they must be considered beneficial from the point of view of human comfort in a land filled with unbelievable numbers of insect pests.

Totem of Three Frogs at Wrangell, Alaska.

LEGEND OF SIX FROGS
Joan Morris
Told by her grandmother

Once upon a time there lived a family at the West Saanich Reserve, near a pond. There were seven children in this family from the ages of seven to fourteen years.

One day they all decided to go hunting together, so they asked permission of their parents.

Just as they were leaving the father took them aside and told them if they stopped at the pond to eat their lunch, they were not to eat anything that they found there. After this they bade farewell to their father and set out in their canoe.

As they were approaching the pond one of them asked if they should stop and eat, as he was very hungry. So they all stopped and ate some of their lunch.

As they were eating one of them noticed a piece of paper with something wrapped inside it. So they all went to see what it was.

When one of the bigger boys opened it they found all sorts of food and dry fish. It looked so delicious that six of the boys started eating, but one of them remembered what his father had told them and he tried to stop his brothers. But they laughed at him and said that he was superstitious, like their father.

Not long after they all felt strange. Then looking at one another they noticed that each one was getting smaller and smaller. Gradually all six of them changed into little green frogs.

The one that did not change got in the canoe and paddled home to tell his father what had happened.

After supper the father told the mother the sad news. Suddenly they heard the croakings of frogs outside and going out they noticed six little frogs. These little frogs stayed there until winter.

That is how the frogs came to the West Saanich Reserve.*

*Saanich Indian reserve near Sidney, Vancouver Island.

Mark Twain's celebrated "The Jumping Frog of Calaveras County" is occasionally revived even in Alaska, as evidenced by the jumping frog contest held at an Anchorage grade school during the summer of 1974 and widely covered in the local press.

Most contemporary superstitions dealing with amphibians and reptiles are false. Toads do not cause warts, salamanders are unable to live in fire and killing a frog does not guarantee rain, as is often alleged. Reptiles have fared even worse than amphibians when it comes to superstitions. Contrary to superstition, however, snakes do not swallow their young in times of danger, nor do they hypnotize potential victims with their lidless stare; and they are not slimy to the touch. Man has little to fear from northern North American amphibians and reptiles. While some frogs, toads and salamanders have skin secretions that are poisonous to small animals, the danger to humans is nonexistent unless the secretion is taken directly into the mouth or eyes, where it can produce a minor, temporary burning sensation.

The bite of the garter snake is *not* poisonous. Most garter snakes refuse to bite but occasionally a freshly caught specimen will bite vigorously. Rarely will such a bite puncture the skin, but if bleeding does occur normal first aid for a minor puncture wound is all that is required. What is more irritating, although equally

ROD BROWN

The Three Frogs at Wrangell in another season.

harmless, is the propensity for freshly caught garter snakes to expel their feces and a foul-smelling fluid from their anal scent glands over the hands of their captor.

Observing and collecting amphibians and their larvae often dictates wading about the margins of small ponds and ditches. Several cases of swimmer's itch (schistosome dermatitis) have been reported from such bodies of water in the Fairbanks area. Swimmer's itch is a skin eruption caused by free-swimming larvae of parasitic worms which attach themselves to the human skin and burrow into it upon emergence from the water. They then die and cause irritation and itching about 4 hours later. Wearing protective boots and vigorously toweling exposed skin immediately upon leaving the water will usually eliminate the possibility of infection.

Occasionally legislators have filed various antisnake measures in the state legislature, hoping to keep Alaska a snakeless state. While the premise that Alaska has no native snakes may be erroneous, there is some merit in restricting importation of exotic animals, including snakes, into a state such as Alaska. More often than not the soon unwanted pet or expended teaching aid is simply released in the backyard to suffer an agonizing death or, in a few remote instances, become established to wreak havoc on populations of native animals.

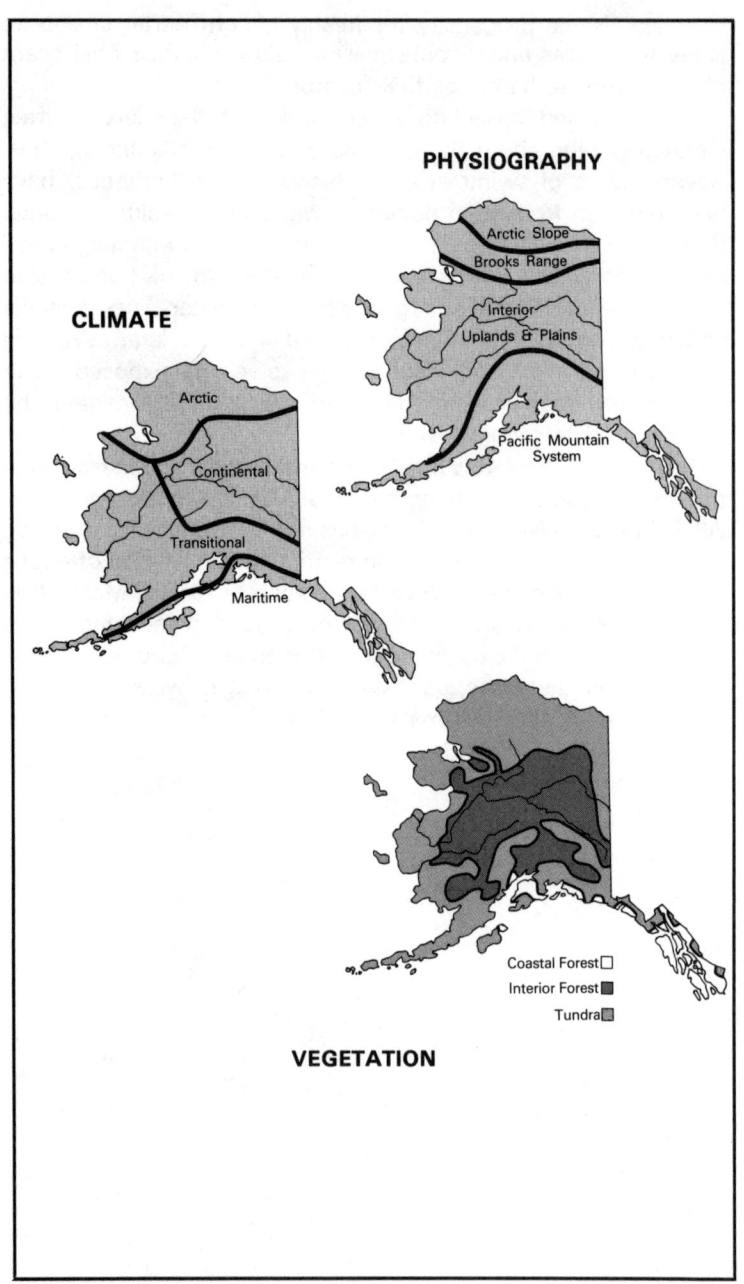

IN ALASKA

PHYSIOGRAPHY, CLIMATE AND VEGETATION OF ALASKA

Alaska is a land of dramatic physical contrasts. It harbors mammoth glaciers, fog-swept fjordlike shores, erupting volcanoes, mighty rivers and endless tundra. The Pacific mountain system stretches in an arc from the Southeastern Panhandle and includes the major ranges of Southcentral and Southwestern Alaska. It gradually diminishes in the Aleutian Chain. Topography is diverse, including the highest mountain in North America and the extensive lowlands of the Cook Inlet basin. Interior uplands and plains make up the largest area in the state, located north and west of the Pacific mountain system, and consist of rolling plains and plateaus drained by the major rivers of the state. The Brooks Range rises abruptly north of the Interior uplands and plains. North of the Brooks Range lies the Arctic Slope with its foothills and vast coastal plain.

The climate of Alaska varies considerably, as the temperature and precipitation figures given here indicate:

	January mean temp.	July mean temp.	Annual precipitation
Ketchikan	35.1°F (1.7°C)	58.0°F (14.4°C)	151.93 in. (385.9 cm)
Anchorage	13.0°F (-10.6°C)	57.3°F (14.1°C)	14.27 in. (36.2 cm)
Fairbanks	-9.8°F (-23.2°C)	60.9°F (16.1°C)	11.92 in. (30.3 cm)
Barrow	-16.2°F (-26.8°C)	33.1°F (0.6°C)	4.26 in. (10.8 cm)

The Southeastern Panhandle and Aleutian Islands have a maritime climate with relatively mild temperatures, much fog and cloudiness, and high precipitation. Southcentral and Southwestern Alaska have a transitional climate with more pronounced temperature variations, less cloudiness, and lower precipitation. The vast Interior has a cold, dry, subarctic or continental climate with severely cold winters and short, occasionally hot, summers. The arctic plains have a somewhat colder and drier climate with moderated extremes.

The vegetation of Alaska, like its climate and physiography, is diverse. Dense coastal forests blanket the steep topography of the Southeastern Panhandle. Taiga, or boreal forest, covers vast areas of the Interior. Tundra gradually replaces taiga in the far northern, western, Aleutian and mountain regions.

The coastal spruce/hemlock forests consist primarily of western hemlock and Sitka spruce with lesser amounts of mountain hemlock, western red cedar, Alaska cedar and black cottonwood. Alder and willow flourish on the banks of streams and rivers. Blueberries, huckleberries, copperbush, devil's club and salal

Southeastern Alaska spruce and hemlock forest near Wrangell.

cover the ground beneath the trees. Throughout the coastal forests, where drainage is poor, treeless bogs called muskegs occur. Muskegs consist of mosses, sedges, rushes and low shrubs.

In the Interior, wherever drainage is good and permafrost lacking, the boreal forest consists primarily of white spruce and paper birch. Balsam poplar, quaking aspen and tamarack are also present in significant numbers. Beneath this canopy, shrubs such as rose, alder and willow occur. Moss usually carpets the floor in profusion.

Interior spruce and birch forest (taiga) near Livengood, Alaska.

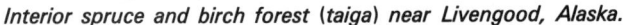

Tundra near Canning River north of Brooks Range, Alaska.

On north-facing slopes and in poorly drained lowlands, usually underlaid by permafrost, black spruce bogs or muskegs are found. Mosses, sedges and low shrubs, along with black spruce, predominate. Throughout the Interior, birch/alder/willow thickets occur near tree line and extend into tundra in many areas.

Where conditions are too severe for tree growth, vast areas of tundra abound. Alpine tundra, consisting of low mat plants, both herbaceous and shrubby, is found on all mountains above the timber line. Wet tundra, consisting primarily of sedges and cottongrass, is found north of the Brooks Range and on the Seward Peninsula; standing water is almost always present in the summer and permafrost is close to the surface. Moist tundra occupies the lower slopes of the Alaska Range, the Aleutian Islands and parts of the Seward Peninsula; cottongrass, tussocks, sedges and dwarf shrubs predominate.

IDENTIFICATION OF ALASKAN AMPHIBIANS. 1 *Spotted frog,* Rana pretiosa, *shows bright salmon red on ventral surfaces.* 2 *Long-toed salamander,* Ambystoma macrodactylum, *has bright yellow, tan or light green dorsal stripe.* 3 *Wood frog,* Rana sylvatica, *has uniformly cream ventral surfaces.* 4 *Northwestern salamander,* Ambystoma gracile, *shows a uniform gray-brown coloration and has sandpaperlike areas on tail and parotoid glands.* 5 *Boreal toad,* Bufo boreas, *is identified by spotted ventral surfaces and squat shape.* 6 *Rough-skinned newt,* Taricha granulosa, *has bright yellow-orange ventral surfaces.*

[1][2] *Wood frogs,* Rana sylvatica, *at Anchorage and Fort Yukon, respectively.* [3] *Boreal toad,* Bufo boreas, *near Juneau.* [4] *Spotted frog,* Rana pretiosa, *in Stikine River area, Alaska.*

[1] *Long-toed salamander,* Ambystoma macrodactylum, *Stikine River, Alaska.* [2] *Northwestern salamander,* Ambystoma gracile, *Kitimat, British Columbia.* [3] *Rough-skinned newt,* Taricha granulosa, *Annette Bay, Alaska.*

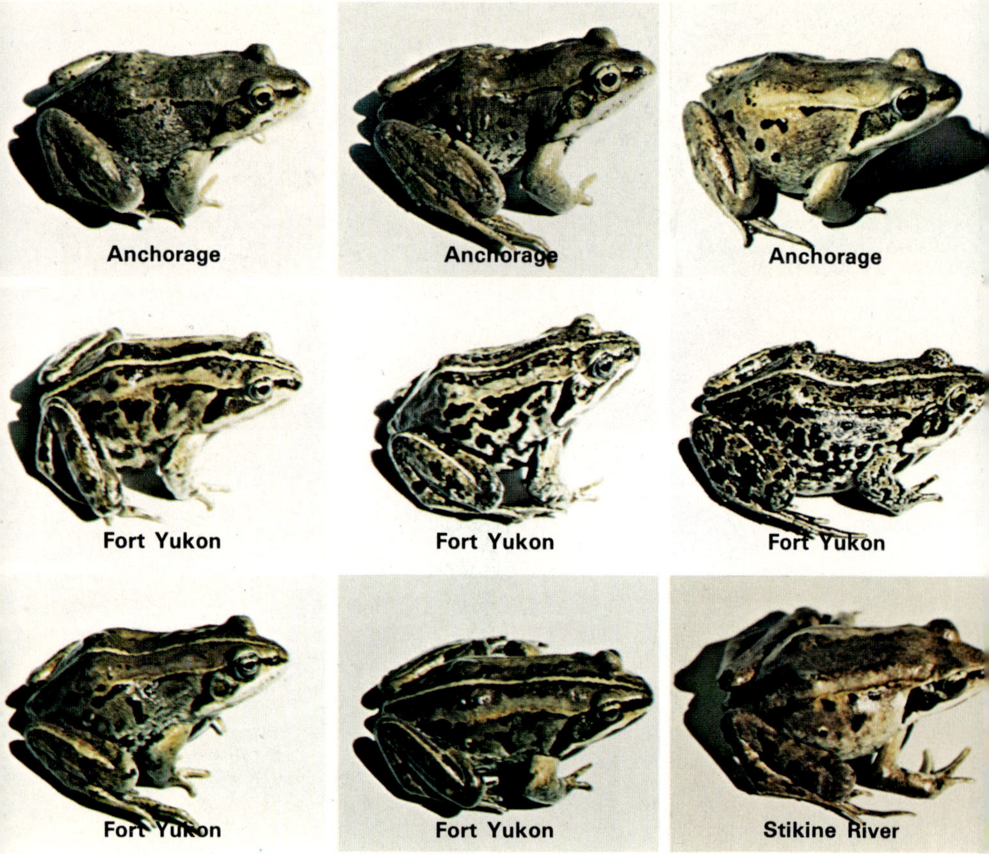

Anchorage　　　Anchorage　　　Anchorage

Fort Yukon　　　Fort Yukon　　　Fort Yukon

Fort Yukon　　　Fort Yukon　　　Stikine River

COLOR VARIATION IN AMPHIBIANS. Both the wood frog (above) and the boreal toad (below) exhibit considerable variation in color and pattern, both in individual populations and from one location to another.

MATING BOREAL TOADS. Having wooed the female to the breeding pond with his mating call, the male toad climbs onto the female's back and grasps her in an embrace called amplexes. Rough patches, called nuptial pads, on the male's forefingers enable him to firmly clasp the female for several hours, occasionally days. So strong is the nuptial embrace that mating pairs can be picked up out of the water and yet remain locked in amplexes. As the stimulated female releases her eggs, aided by her mate's squeezing embrace, the male floods the emerging eggs with sperm.

Evident in these photographs are the smooth appearance of the breeding male's skin, the large size and rough skin texture of the gravid female, and two strings of eggs, one from each ovary, leaving the female's body. Females of some species carry as many as 30,000 eggs.

IDENTIFICATION OF CANADIAN AMPHIBIANS. Note the color variations within each species. [1][2] Leopard frog, *Rana pipiens,* is distinguished by light-bordered dark spots on dorsal surfaces. [3] The Candian toad, *Bufo hemiophrys,* has a prominent ridge between the eyes. [4][5] Chorus frog, *Pseudacris triseriata,* is small and has stripes from nose to vent. [6][7] Wood frog, *Rana sylvatica,* has a usually prominent, dark, eye mask and uniformly cream-colored ventral surfaces. [8][9] Hudson Bay toad, *Bufo americanus,* has vivid coloration and narrow parotoid glands.

[1] *Common garter snake,* Thamnophis sirtalis, *from Salt River, Northwest Territories.* [2] *Leopard frog,* Rana pipiens, *and* [3] *chorus frog,* Pseudacris triseriata, *both from Moosonee, Ontario, near James Bay.*

1 *Canadian toad,* Bufo hemiophrys, *at Red Deer River, Alberta.* 2 *Hudson Bay toad,* Bufo americanus, *observed at Moosonee, Ontario, near James Bay.*

CHECK LIST OF SPECIES PRESENT IN ALASKA

All organisms are classified scientifically in a hierarchy based on structural and evolutionary relationships. Alaskan species of amphibians are classified as follows:

Kingdom: Animalia (animals)
  Phylum: Chordata (chordates)
    Class: Amphibia (frogs, toads, salamanders, caecillians)
      Order: Caudata (salamanders)
        Family: Salamandridae (newts)
          Genus: *Taricha* (rough-skinned newt, etc.)
            Species: *Taricha granulosa* (rough-skinned newt)
        Family: Ambystomidae (mole salamanders)
          Genus: *Ambystoma* (long-toed salamander, northwestern salamander, etc.)
            Species: *Ambystoma macrodactylum* (long-toed salamander)
            Ambystoma gracile (northwestern salamander)
      Order: Anura (frogs and toads)
        Family: Bufonidae (toads)
          Genus: *Bufo* (boreal toad, Canadian toad)
            Species: *Bufo boreas* (boreal toad)
        Family: Ranidae (true frogs)
          Genus: *Rana* (wood frog, spotted frog, leopard frog, etc.)
            Species: *Rana sylvatica* (wood frog)
            Rana pretiosa (spotted frog)

ROUGH-SKINNED NEWT
Taricha granulosa

Taricha is from the Greek tarichos meaning mummy; *granulosa* means granulation.

DISTINGUISHING CHARACTERS
Rough skin (except in breeding male) and bright yellow/orange on ventral surfaces.

DESCRIPTION
A rough-skinned brown salamander with bright yellow/orange on ventral surfaces. Breeding male has smooth skin, swollen vent and forelimbs, flattened tail, and dark pads on feet. No costal grooves. To 6 inches (15 centimeters).

DISTRIBUTION IN ALASKA
Coastal forests (spruce and hemlock) from Cook Inlet to the British Columbia border.

HABITAT
Aquatic. Found in and about small permanent bodies of water with abundant vegetation.

POSTGLACIAL DISPERSAL
Present distribution suggests survival in the Pacific Refuge, entering Alaska via the coastal corridor.

REMARKS
Most abundant of the tailed amphibians. Diurnal and often seen. The lizard of the totem carver. Evidently Alaskan larvae require 2 years to complete metamorphosis. Both adults and larvae can be readily observed in suitable ponds throughout the summer.

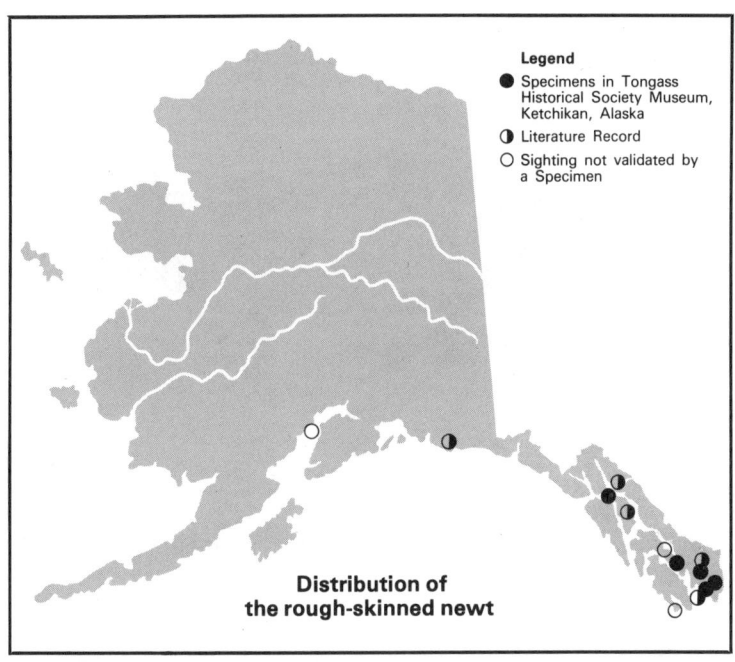

Breeding ponds of the rough-skinned newt near Ward Lake, about 5 miles northwest of Ketchikan, Alaska.

NORTHWESTERN SALAMANDER
Ambystoma gracile

Ambystoma refers to the rounded cuplike mouth and *gracile* means slender or slim.

DISTINGUISHING CHARACTERS
Sandpaperlike areas on tail and parotoid glands and uniform gray-brown coloration.

DESCRIPTION
A large, robust, smooth-skinned, uniformly gray-brown salamander with pitted granular areas on tail and parotoid glands. Milk-white flecks may be present on dorsal surfaces. Costal grooves. To 6 inches (15 centimeters).

DISTRIBUTION IN ALASKA
Coastal forests of extreme Southeastern Alaska.

HABITAT
Found under rocks, boards, and rotting logs in forested areas adjacent to fresh water. Breeds in muskeg ponds and lakes.

POSTGLACIAL DISPERSAL
Present distribution suggests survival of glaciation in Pacific Refuge and dispersal to Alaska via coastal corridor.

REMARKS
Nocturnal and secretive. Seldom seen except during the short early spring breeding season. Green algae are often present in the firm globular egg mass. Alaskan larvae apparently require 2 years to complete metamorphosis. A white, mildly toxic, milky fluid is secreted from the granular areas of this salamander when molested.

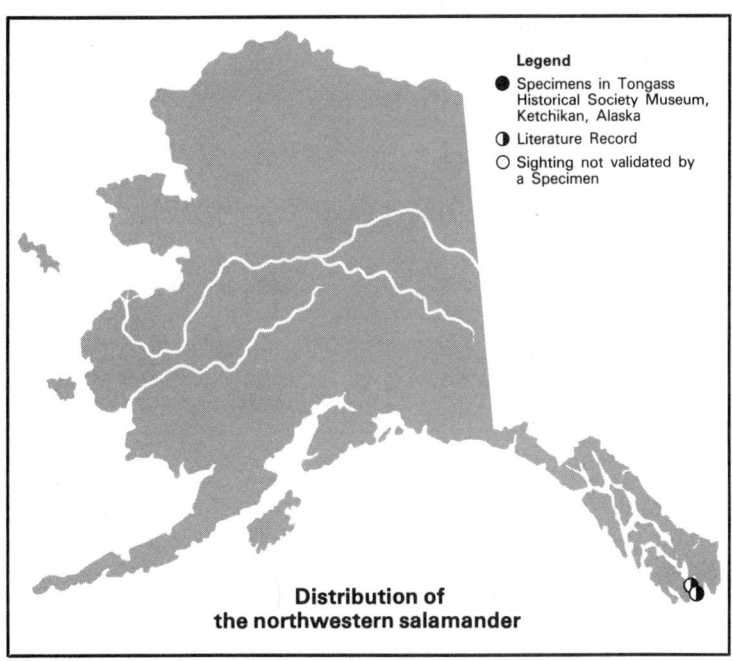

Legend
● Specimens in Tongass Historical Society Museum, Ketchikan, Alaska
◐ Literature Record
○ Sighting not validated by a Specimen

Distribution of the northwestern salamander

Small pond on Mary Island, Alaska, similar to ponds near Kitimat, British Columbia, where the northwestern salamander breeds.

LONG-TOED SALAMANDER
Ambystoma macrodactylum

Ambystoma refers to the rounded cuplike mouth and *macrodactylum* means long finger.

DISTINGUISHING CHARACTERS
Bright yellow, tan or light green dorsal stripe.
DESCRIPTION
A delicate, smooth-skinned dusky or black salamander with an irregular yellow, tan or light green dorsal stripe. White flecking on sides. Ventral surface gray. Long toes. Faint costal grooves. To 5 inches (13 centimeters).
DISTRIBUTION IN ALASKA
Southeastern coastal forests adjacent to the Stikine and Taku rivers.
HABITAT
Terrestrial. Adults enter water only during the early spring breeding season. Found under boards, logs and ground litter in forested areas adjacent to fresh water.
POSTGLACIAL DISPERSAL
Present distribution of this salamander suggests survival during glaciation in the Pacific Refuge, entering Alaska via the intermountain corridor (between the Coast and Rocky Mountains of British Columbia) and through the Coast Mountains via the Stikine and Taku rivers. The coastal form of this salamander is found as far north as Kitimat, British Columbia, suggesting the possibility of two routes of entry into the state.
REMARKS
Breeds in early spring when ponds are not completely free of ice. Eggs deposited in small, jelly-coated masses. Larvae may overwinter in Alaska. Nocturnal and secretive.

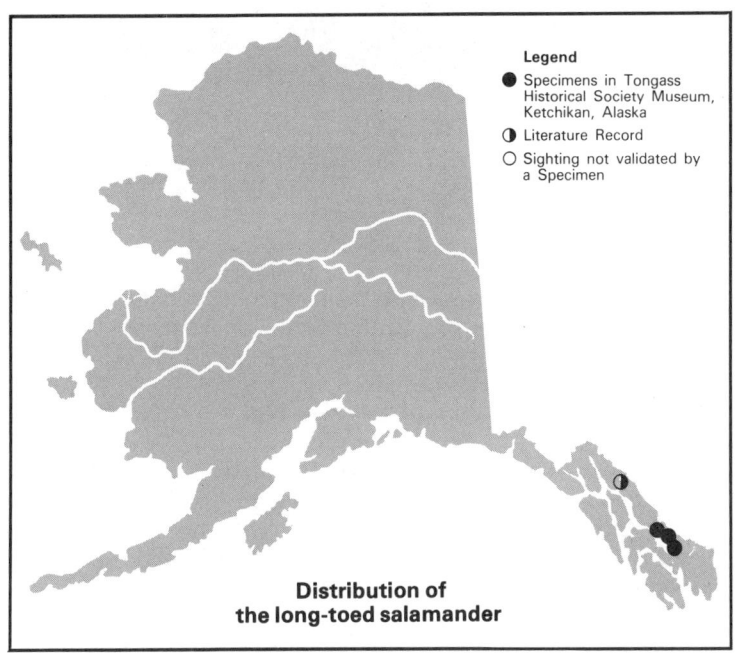

Distribution of the long-toed salamander

Habitat of the long-toed salamander at Twin Lakes on the Stikine River, Alaska.

BOREAL TOAD
Bufo boreas

Bufo is after the Latin *bufonis,* meaning toad, and *boreas* means the north wind, pertaining to the north, or northern.

DISTINGUISHING CHARACTERS
Dry, warty appearance of the skin and the squat shape.
DESCRIPTION
A chunky, short-legged, warty amphibian with dominant parotoid glands. Ground color is brown, green or gray with dark blotches. Undersurfaces white with black mottling. A dominant white or cream-colored vertebral stripe is usually evident. To 3½ inches (9 centimeters).
DISTRIBUTION IN ALASKA
Coastal forests in Southeastern and Southcentral Alaska from Prince William Sound south to the British Columbia border.
HABITAT
Terrestrial. Generally found in open, nonforested areas adjacent to fresh water. Breeds in muskeg ponds, streams, rain pools and ditches.
VOICE
Breeding call is a soft birdlike clucking.
POSTGLACIAL DISPERSAL
The present distribution of *Bufo boreas* suggests this toad survived glaciation in the Pacific Refuge. It appears to have entered Alaska via the coastal corridor. It may also have entered the state via the Stikine River.
REMARKS
Abundant and often seen. Active during daylight hours. The frog of the totem carver. Often walks rather than hops. Breeds May-July in Juneau area. Eggs deposited in rosarylike strings. Tadpoles black, young toadlets often less than ½ inch long (1.3 centimeters) at transformation. Waves of metamorphosing toads are readily observed during July-August in small ponds in the Juneau area. The pond margins are often so littered with minute toadlets that it is impossible to take a step without crushing several individuals. These same ponds still contain

numerous tadpoles, many without legs yet developed, indicating mating and egg deposition may extend for some period of time. Also, certain individuals of each batch of tadpoles grow rapidly at first, releasing a growth-inhibiting substance which acts upon the smaller tadpoles, resulting in metamorphosis in waves rather than all at once. Mass mortality due to predation or unfavorable environmental conditions in the terrestrial environment at the time of metamorphosis is therefore prevented.

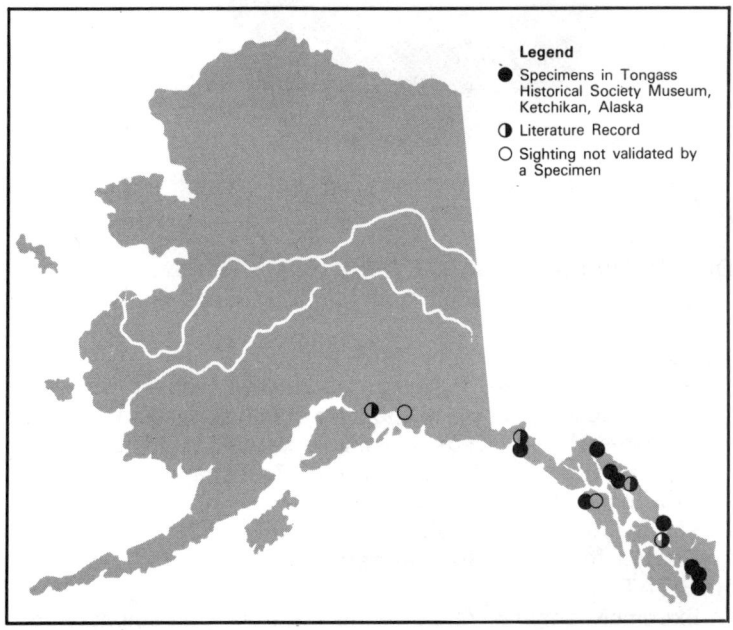

Breeding pond of the boreal toad near Yakutat, Alaska.

SPOTTED FROG
Rana pretiosa

Rana has a Sanskrit root meaning one uttering a sound, and *pretiosa* means precious.

DISTINGUISHING CHARACTERS
Large size as an adult and bright salmon red on ventral surfaces.
DESCRIPTION
A smooth-skinned, light or dark brown, robust frog with numerous irregular black spots on dorsal surfaces. Prominent dorsolateral folds. Legs indistinctly banded. Undersurface of legs and stomach bright salmon red. Light stripe on jaw. Adults to 3 inches (7.6 centimeters).
DISTRIBUTION IN ALASKA
Coastal forests of Southeastern Alaska.
HABITAT
Extremely aquatic, rarely found far from permanent water. Frequents the grassy margins of streams, rivers and lakes.
VOICE
A low basslike drone often emitted while under water.
POSTGLACIAL DISPERSAL
Present distribution suggests this frog survived glaciation in the Pacific Refuge east of the Cascade Mountains and entered Alaska via the intermontane corridor between the Coast and Rocky Mountains of British Columbia, crossing the Coast Mountains via the major rivers of the area.
REMARKS
A very active robust frog. Spends the entire summer in or near permanent water.

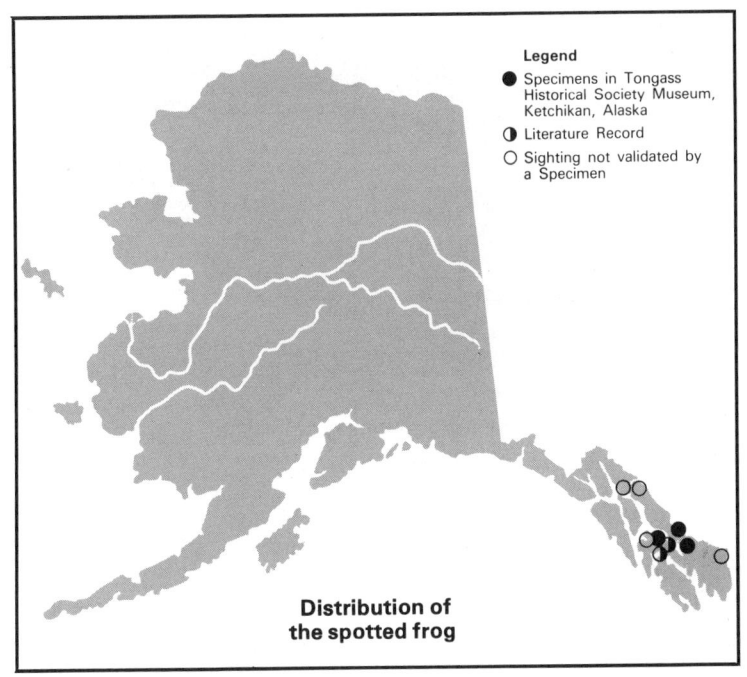

Habitat of the spotted frog at Twin Lakes on the Stikine River, Alaska.

WOOD FROG
Rana sylvatica

Rana has a Sanskrit root meaning one uttering a sound and *sylvatica* means living among trees.

DISTINGUISHING CHARACTERS
Usually prominent, dark eye mask and the uniformly cream ventral surfaces.

DESCRIPTION
A smooth-skinned, light brown or gray frog with a usually prominent dark eye mask. Light vertebral stripe often present. Numerous dark spots often present on dorsal surface of northern forms. Undersurfaces uniformly cream white. Adults to 3 inches (7.6 centimeters).

DISTRIBUTION IN ALASKA
Widespread throughout the state and has been observed north of the Brooks Range.

HABITAT
Found in forest, muskeg and tundra. Breeds in early spring in shallow bodies of water. A resident of grassland and open forest, often found considerable distances from water.

VOICE
A rapidly repeated ducklike staccato.

POSTGLACIAL DISPERSAL
Present distribution suggests survival during glaciation in widely scattered areas, south and, speculatively, north (Bering Refuge) of the glacier margins. The morphological differences of a species may be interpreted in terms of geographic isolation in several glacial refuges. We can theorize that the Alaskan wood frog, the old *Rana sylvatica latiremis,* survived glaciation in the Bering Refuge with subsequent dispersal throughout Alaska and the Yukon and Northwest Territories and then

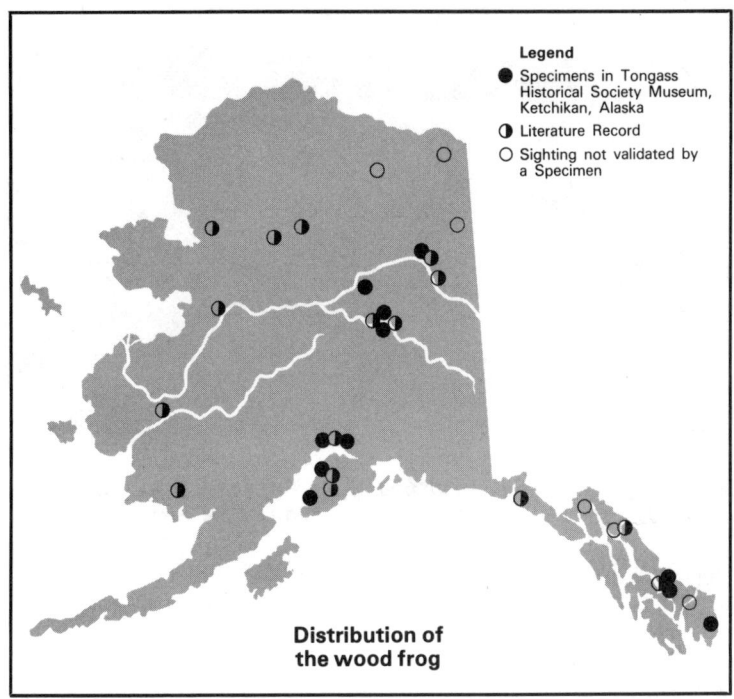

Distribution of the wood frog

southeastward, where it met (in an area from central British Columbia through Alberta, Saskatchewan, Manitoba and extreme northwestern Ontario) northward dispersing forms that survived glaciation south of the glacier margins.

REMARKS

Abundant. Active at temperatures barely above freezing. Breeds in early spring (April-June in Interior Alaska). Eggs are deposited in masses slightly beneath the water surface. Tadpole development is rapid, metamorphosis normally occurring well before autumn freezeup. Present studies indicate a terrestrial hibernation site, and the use of physiochemical mechanisms for protection against extreme cold and dryness.

Breeding ponds of the wood frog: [1] At Earthquake Park, Anchorage, Alaska. [2] Near Fort Yukon, Alaska, just north of the Arctic Circle.

OTHER SPECIES THAT MAY BE PRESENT IN ALASKA

The status of the Alaskan worm salamander, *Batrachoseps caudatus,* needs verification. This can be accomplished only by intensive searching throughout Southeastern Alaska, Annette Island and Yakutat in particular. If, in fact, worm salamanders exist in Alaska, exactly when these subterranean dwellers are active on the surface—readily observable—remains to be determined. The fact that Nichols (the collector of the original specimen) was at Hassler Harbor in August might indicate surface activity.

Other species of amphibians may eventually be found in Alaska. The chorus frog, *Pseudacris triseriata,* is widely distributed east of the Rocky Mountains and has ascended the Liard River as far as Fort Nelson, British Columbia. It is but a short distance from the Liard River headwaters to the Yukon River headwaters. Whether this frog has extended or is extending its range into the Yukon Territory and Alaska via the Yukon River deserves investigation.

Salamanders of the genus *Hynobius* are widespread throughout Eurasia. The Siberian salamander, *Hynobius keyserlingi,* has an extensive range throughout northern Eurasia and is found farther north than any other salamander. It is tempting to speculate that the range of *Hynobius* at one time included Alaska, when Asian and North American forests were connected, and that relict populations might still exist in the state. Perhaps, as previously

SMITHSONIAN INSTITUTION

Alaskan worm salamander collected in 1882 at Hassler Harbor, Annette Island, Alaska.

discussed, cold-adapted amphibians like *Hynobius* and *Rana sylvatica* found refuge in the pockets of woodland that remained in the ice-free areas of Alaska during Pleistocene glaciation. Salamanders of the family *Hynobiidae* are the only group of salamanders not represented in the New World. They have long been in a position to make the crossing, but until someone finds a Siberian salamander somewhere in Alaska, we must assume they have not. Several authors have suggested the North American ambystomid salamanders evolved from the hynobids, which might explain the problem.

The status of Alaska's lone reptile, the garter snake, like the worm salamander, needs verification. While three reliable sight records exist (including an actual specimen which resided for a time in the old Territorial Museum in Juneau) we know nothing about snakes in Alaska other than that three separate people, including two federal biologists, have observed snakes on the banks of the Taku River and the Stikine River. Because the locations of the three sightings are remote from human habitation, we can assume these snakes reached Alaska naturally. All other references to snakes in the state which have occasionally appeared in the press have been located at or near human population centers. The snakes appear to have been individuals unintentionally released from cargo shipments originating outside Alaska or escapees from carnivals and road shows.

Thamnophis sirtalis, the garter snake, is widely distributed throughout British Columbia. It is common in the Coast Mountains as far north as Terrace and has been reported from Mile 125 on the Alaska Highway, just 200 miles (320 kilometers) as the crow flies, south of the Yukon border. Apparently the three legitimate sightings in Alaska are the result of snakes entering Southeastern Alaska via the major rivers that slice through the Coast Mountains.

Whether garter snakes are established (have breeding populations) in Alaska remains to be determined. As previously noted, the two reptiles found above the Arctic Circle in Scandinavia, the lizard *Lacerta vivipara,* and the adder *Vipera berus,* are both viviparous and have made the necessary adaptations for northern survival. North American garter snakes are also viviparous but it is not presently known if they exhibit similar behavioral and developmental adaptations in the

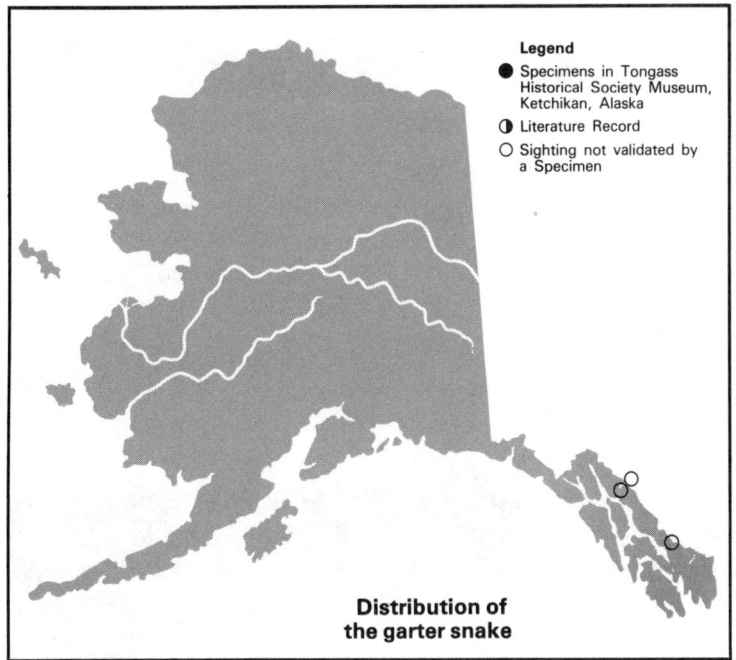

Distribution of the garter snake

northernmost forms. Even so, the climate of Southeastern Alaska, which differs significantly from arctic Scandinavia, might prove detrimental to a reptile. While the long summer days of arctic Norway are filled with abundant sunshine and little rain, the significantly shorter days of Southeastern Alaska have considerably more rainfall and much cloud cover, with a resulting reduction in necessary sunshine.

Occasionally the giant tropical marine turtles wander far to the north and are sighted offshore, some occasionally grounding on northern beaches. The large leatherback turtle, *Dermochelys coriacea* (to 8 feet, or 2.4 meters), has been recorded north of the Arctic Circle off the coast of Scandinavia. This species has recently been shown to have a mammal-like ability to maintain a high body temperature (about 80° F, or 27° C). In North America it is occasionally sighted off the coast of British Columbia as far north as the Queen Charlotte Islands. The green turtle, *Chelonia mydas* (to 5 feet, or 1.5 meters), has been recorded from Vancouver Island, British Columbia.

Taiga near Great Slave Lake in the Northwest Territories.

IN THE YUKON & NORTHWEST TERRITORIES

> *What a queer bird the frog are!*
> *When he sit he stand—almost;*
> *When he walk he fly—almost;*
> *When he sing he cry—almost;*
> *He ain't got no sense—hardly;*
> *He ain't got no tail—hardly, either;*
> *He sit on what he ain't got—almost.*
>
> Anonymous French Canadian
> In THE COMING OF THE POND FISHES
> by Ben Hur Lampman

The Yukon and Northwest Territories, like Alaska, are a vast northern region with a hostile climate and few amphibians and reptiles. Only two amphibians are widely distributed in the territories. However, as in Alaska, more southern climatic and vegetational influences reach the territories in a few areas and bring a few additional amphibians and reptiles north of 60° latitude.

The wood frog is found throughout the taiga and adjacent tundra of the Yukon and Northwest Territories. The only other amphibian or reptile with an extensive distribution north of 60° latitude is the chorus frog, which is found in the Northwest Territories from Great Bear Lake south to the provincial borders. The mixed wood forest (boreal forest, aspen groves, grassland) extends northward to the area around Fort Smith which straddles the Northwest Territories/Alberta border. This prairie influence brings the leopard frog, Canadian toad and garter snake into the territory.

Postglacial dispersal of the wood frog has already been discussed. Apparently the remaining amphibians and reptiles of the Northwest Territories, (except for those of the islands in James Bay) survived glaciation in forests just south of the glacier margins or in prairies in what now is the southwestern United States.

PHYSIOGRAPHY, CLIMATE AND VEGETATION OF THE YUKON AND NORTHWEST TERRITORIES

Also like Alaska, the Yukon and Northwest Territories north of 60° latitude exhibit diverse land forms. Most of the Yukon and the extreme western areas of the Northwest Territories are covered with mountains. These mountains, which include the highest peak in Canada, gradually diminish into a broad flat northward extension of the western plains, which is drained by the Mackenzie River. The Canadian Shield, an area of low topography, exposed rocks, and numerous ponds and lakes, is adjacent to the western plains. To the north and east is the Arctic Coast. It is a region of low relief except for mountainous areas on Ellesmere, Baffin and Victoria Islands.

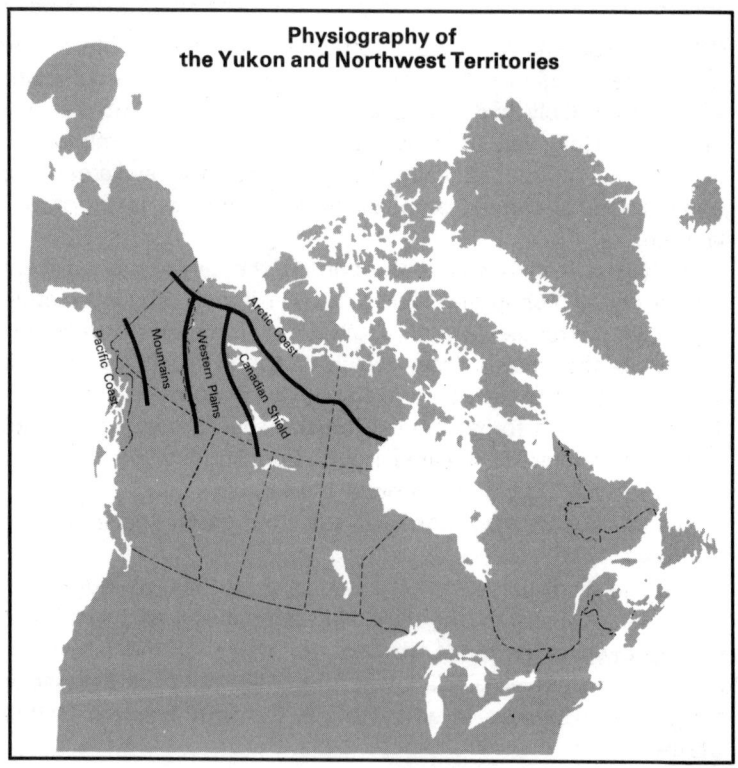

The vegetation of the lower elevations of the mountains, western plains and Canadian Shield consists of taiga, similar to Interior Alaska. Predominant species include black and white spruce, aspen, birch, poplar, tamarack and pine. Tundra gradually replaces taiga at high elevations and on the Arctic Coast.

Most of the Yukon and Northwest Territories have a subarctic climate with cold winters and short, cool summers:

	January mean temp.	July mean temp.	Annual precipitation
Yellowknife, NWT	-19.4°F (-28.6°C)	60.8°F (16.0°C)	9.8 in. (25.0 cm)
Whitehorse, YT	-5.0°F (-20.6°C)	56.0°F (13.3°C)	11.0 in. (27.9 cm)

The northern coastal areas and islands have an arctic climate with severely cold winters and extremely short, cool summers.

During the Pleistocene period the Northwest Territories and most of the Yukon were completely covered by ice. The ice sheet remained in the eastern area of the Canadian north long after it had retreated from more southern and western areas.

JAMES BAY

James Bay, the southern extension of Hudson Bay, penetrates southward into Ontario and Quebec to 51° north latitude. It shares many similarities, geological, floral and faunal with these two provinces. Charlton Island, the southernmost major island in James Bay, is much farther south than the southern tip of the Alaska Panhandle and lies at the approximate latitude of the city of Saskatoon, Saskatchewan, and only 200 miles (320 kilometers) north of northernmost Minnesota. But since all offshore islands within James Bay are politically part of the Northwest Territories (District of Keewatin), they may appropriately be considered here.

The major islands in James Bay include Akimiski, the largest, with an area of 1,137 square miles; Charlton, the other large island; North Twin; South Twin; Cape Hope; Strutton; Trodley; Danby; Carey; Weston; Jacob; Spence; Grey Goose; and Bear. These islands are considered part of the Canadian Shield and consist of low, flat, swampy remnants of the interior plains now referred to as the Hudson Bay lowlands. Akimiski, Charlton, Cape Hope, Strutton, Trodley, Danby, and Carey Islands support

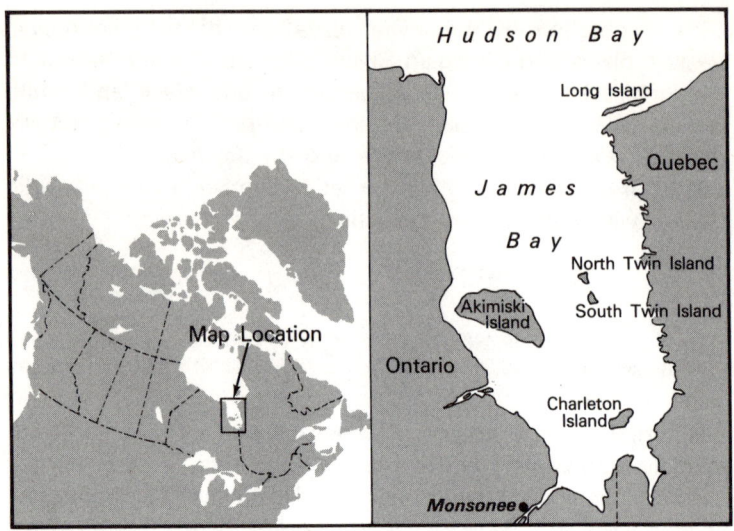

Although considerably south of 60 degrees north latitude, all the islands in James Bay are politically part of the Northwest Territories.

considerable forest cover, consisting of black and white spruce, willow, aspen, alder, poplar and birch. Tundra blankets the small northern islands. The climate of the area is subarctic, Hudson Bay pushing severe climatic conditions farther south than at any other point in North America. Hudson Bay remains ice-covered well into summer, serving to lower temperatures considerably during the critical spring growing season on islands and the adjacent mainland. Severe winds and fog are also significant factors throughout the warm months. Pleistocene glaciation completely covered the James Bay region.

A few herpetological investigations have been made on the Ontario/Quebec mainland around James Bay but little, if any, herpetological work has been accomplished on the islands within James Bay. Amphibians and reptiles recorded from the islands in James Bay include the Hudson Bay toad, *Bufo americanus,* from Akimiski and Cape Hope Islands; the chorus frog, *Pseudacris triseriata,* from Akimiski Island; and the wood frog, *Rana sylvatica,* from Akimiski and Cape Hope Islands.

The extent of distribution of the amphibians and reptiles in James Bay remains to be determined. It is generally believed that most of the cold-tolerant, boreal amphibians and reptiles now found in the James Bay region found shelter during glaciation just south of the glacier margins and/or in the Appalachian Mountain Refuge, with subsequent dispersal northward following closely behind the retreat of the glaciers.

CHECK LIST OF SPECIES PRESENT IN THE YUKON AND NORTHWEST TERRITORIES

All organisms are classified scientifically in a hierarchy based on structural and evolutionary relationships. The species of amphibians and reptiles present in the Yukon and Northwest Territories are classified as follows:

Kingdom: Animalia (animals)
  Phylum: Chordata (chordates)
    Class: Amphibia (frogs, toads, salamanders, caecilians)
      Order: Anura (frogs and toads)
        Family: Bufonidae (toads)
          Genus: *Bufo* (boreal toad, Canadian toad, etc.)
            Species: *Bufo hemiophrys* (Canadian toad)
                Bufo americanus
                (Hudson Bay toad)
        Family: Hylidae (tree toads)
          Genus: *Pseudacris* (chorus frogs)
            Species: *Pseudacris triseriata* (chorus frog)
        Family: Ranidae (true frogs)
          Genus: *Rana* (wood frog, spotted frog,
            leopard frog, etc.)
            Species: *Rana sylvatica* (wood frog)
                Rana pipiens (leopard frog)
    Class: Reptilia (turtles, tuatara, crocodiles,
      lizards, snakes)
      Order: Serpentes (snakes)
        Family: Colubridae (colubrid snakes)
          Genus: *Thamnophis* (garter snakes)
            Species: *Thamnophis sirtalis*
                (common garter snake)

CANADIAN TOAD
Bufo hemiophrys

Bufo is after the Latin *bufonis,* meaning toad, and *hemiophrys* means inseparable brow or eyebrow.

DISTINGUISHING CHARACTERS
   Prominent ridge between eyes.
DESCRIPTION
   A dry-looking, warty toad with rusty brown or greenish skin. Vertebral stripe often present. Prominent ridge between eyes. To 3 inches (7.6 centimeters).
DISTRIBUTION IN NORTHWEST TERRITORIES
   Fort Smith area of the Northwest Territories.
HABITAT
   Grassy margins of prairie lakes, ponds and ditches.
VOICE
   A soft trill.
REMARKS
   Diurnal, eggs deposited in strings, tadpoles black.

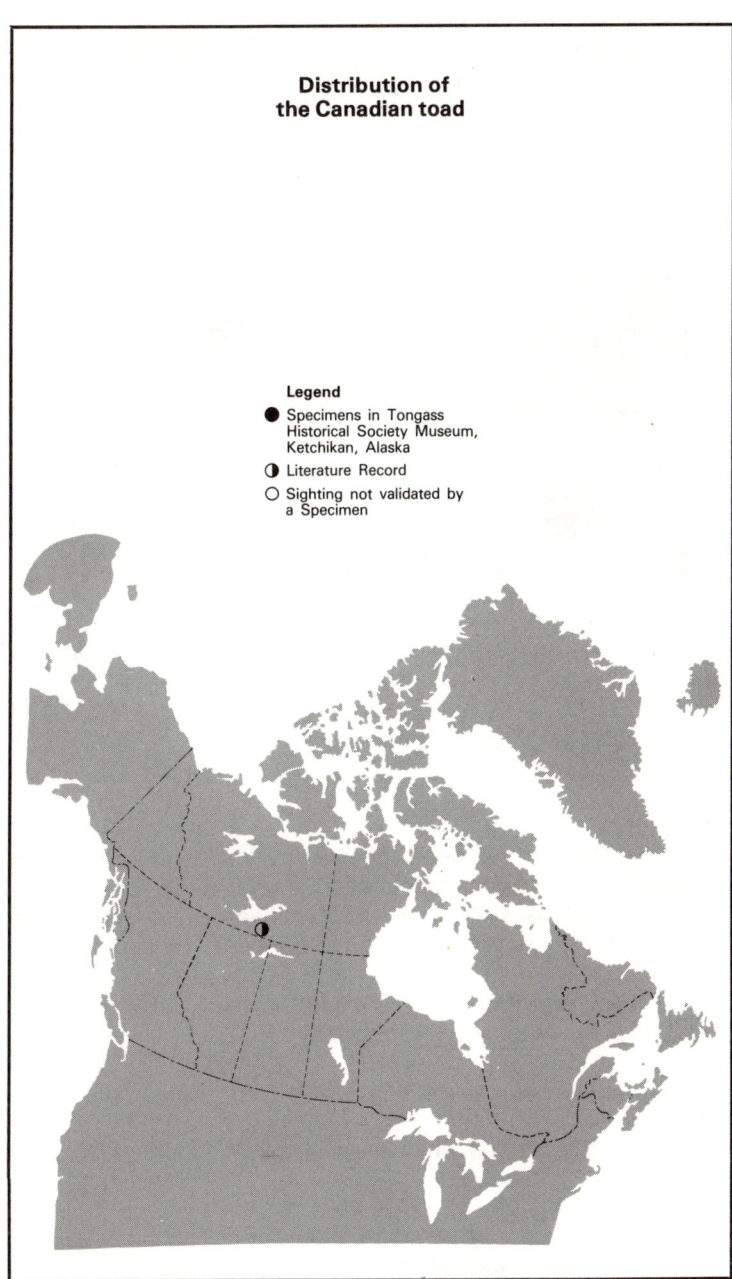

Distribution of the Canadian toad

Legend
● Specimens in Tongass Historical Society Museum, Ketchikan, Alaska
◐ Literature Record
○ Sighting not validated by a Specimen

HUDSON BAY TOAD (American Toad)
Bufo americanus

Bufo is after the Latin *bufonis,* meaning toad, and *americanus* refers to America.

DISTINGUISHING CHARACTERS
　Narrow paratoid glands, vivid coloration, white dorsolateral stripe.

DESCRIPTION
　An intensely colored dry-skinned warty toad with long narrow parotoid glands. Dorsal coloration is vivid black, brown, red, white and pink with a broad prominent white dorsolateral stripe. Ventral surface mottled. To 3 inches (7.6 centimeters).

DISTRIBUTION
　Recorded from Akimiski Island and the Cape Hope Islands in James Bay, Northwest Territories.

HABITAT
　Open grassy areas adjacent to fresh-water ponds and lakes.

VOICE
　A prolonged, high-pitched musical trill commonly lasting 30 seconds.

REMARKS
　A vividly marked northern form of the common toad of eastern Canada and United States.

CHORUS FROG
Pseudacris triseriata

←——— 1 inch ———→
(2.5 centimeters)

Pseudacris is after the Greek *pseudes,* false, and *acris* meaning a locust. *Triseriata* means three stripes.

DISTINGUISHING CHARACTERS
Small size as adult, stripes from nose to vent.
DESCRIPTION
A minute delicate frog with a pointed head and long toes with enlarged discs on the digits. Gray with brown stripes from nose to vent. Adult to 1 inch (2.5 centimeters).
DISTRIBUTION IN NORTHWEST TERRITORIES
The Northwest Territories from Great Bear Lake south to British Columbia, Alberta, Saskatchewan and Manitoba borders.
HABITAT
Grassy margins of lakes and marshes.
VOICE
An intense vibrating "preep."
REMARKS
Often heard but rarely seen due to its small size and protective coloration. Eggs laid in small clusters, tadpoles transform at ½ inch.

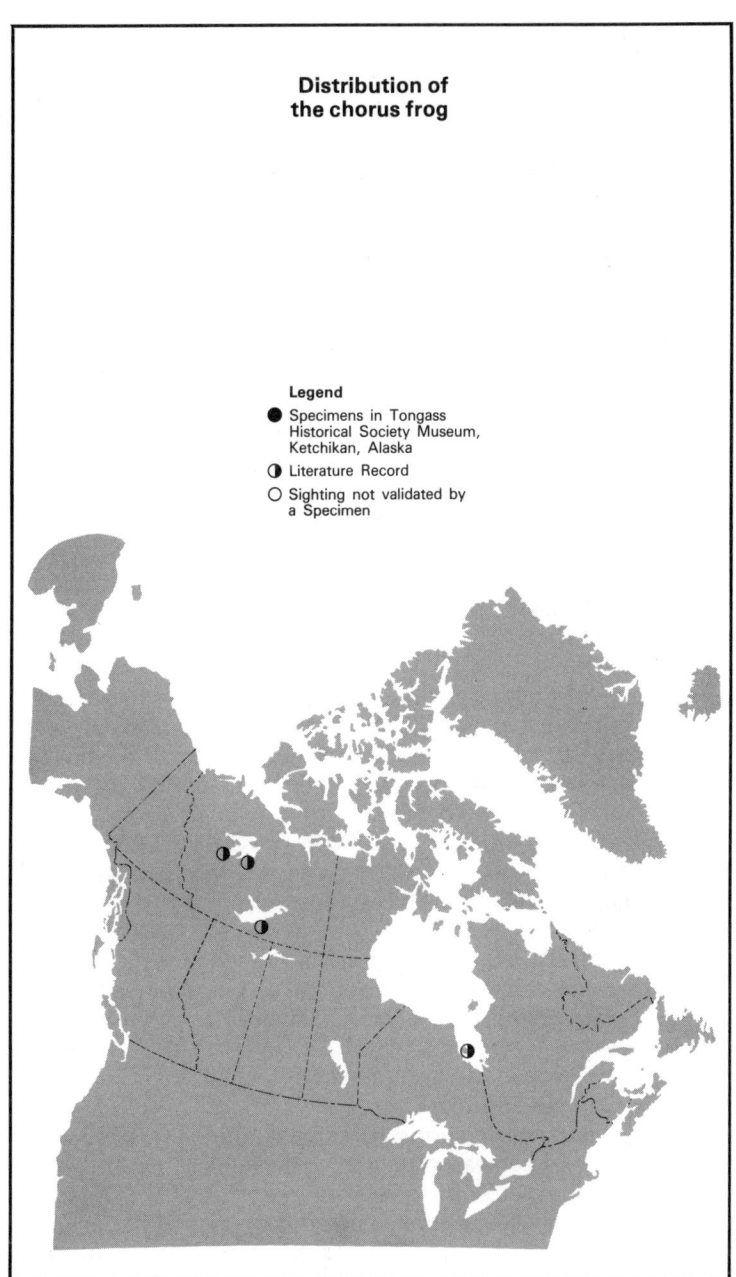

WOOD FROG
Rana sylvatica

At Whitehorse, Yukon Territory

At Hay River, Northwest Territories

Rana has a Sanskrit root meaning one uttering a sound and *sylvatica* means living among trees.

DISTINGUISHING CHARACTERS
Usually prominent, dark eye mask and the uniformly cream ventral surfaces.

DESCRIPTION
A smooth-skinned, light brown or gray frog with a usually prominent dark eye mask. Light vertebral stripe often present. Numerous dark spots often present on dorsal surface of northern forms. Undersurfaces uniformly cream white. Adults to 3 inches (7.6 centimeters).

DISTRIBUTION IN YUKON AND NORTHWEST TERRITORIES
Found throughout the forested areas and adjacent tundra of the Yukon and Northwest Territories.

HABITAT
Found in forest, muskeg and tundra. Breeds in early spring in shallow bodies of water. A resident of grassland and open forest, often found considerable distances from water.

VOICE
A rapidly repeated ducklike staccato.

POSTGLACIAL DISPERSAL
Present distribution suggests survival during glaciation in widely scattered areas, south and, speculatively, north (Bering Refuge) of the glacier margins. The morphological differences of a species may be interpreted in terms of geographic isolation in several glacial refuges. We can theorize that the Alaskan wood frog, the old *Rana sylvatica latiremis,* survived glaciation

in the Bering Refuge with subsequent dispersal throughout Alaska and the Yukon and Northwest Territories and then southeastward, where it met (in an area from central British Columbia through Alberta, Saskatchewan, Manitoba and extreme northwestern Ontario) northward dispersing forms that survived glaciation south of the glacier margins.

REMARKS

Abundant. Active at temperatures barely above freezing. Breeds in early spring (April-June in Interior Alaska). Eggs are deposited in masses slightly beneath the water surface. Tadpole development is rapid, metamorphosis normally occurring well before autumn freezeup. Present studies indicate a terrestrial hibernation site, and the use of physiochemical mechanisms for protection against extreme cold and dryness.

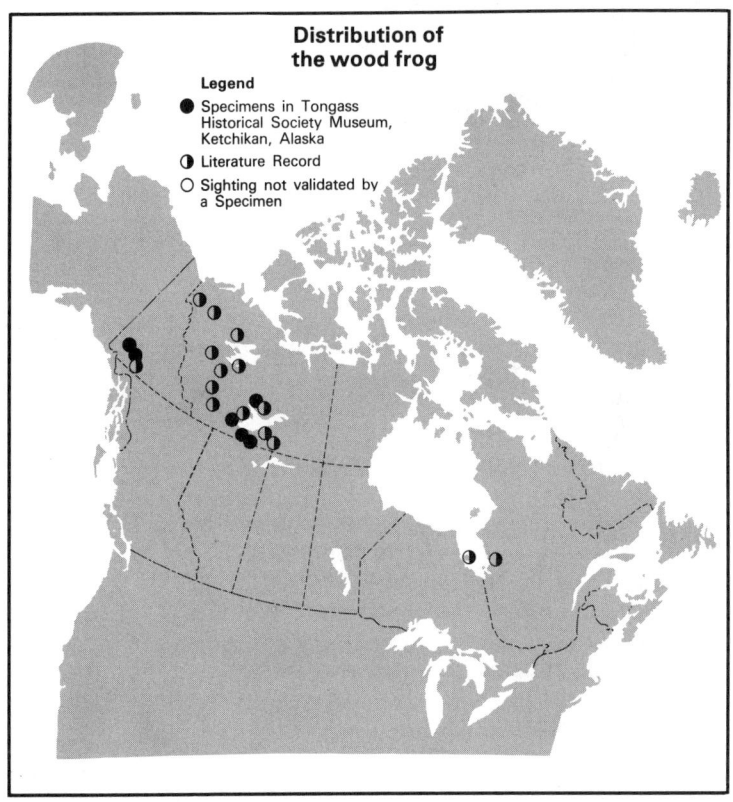

LEOPARD FROG
Rana pipiens

Rana has a Sanskrit root meaning one uttering a sound and *pipiens* means peeping.

DISTINGUISHING CHARACTERS
  Light bordered dark spots.
DESCRIPTION
  A smooth-skinned, green or brown frog with light bordered dark spots. To 3 inches (7.6 centimeters).
DISTRIBUTION IN NORTHWEST TERRITORIES
  Fort Smith area of the Northwest Territories
HABITAT
  Margins of streams, marshes and lakes.
VOICE
  A deep clacking.
REMARKS
  Eggs deposited in flattened masses, tadpoles large.

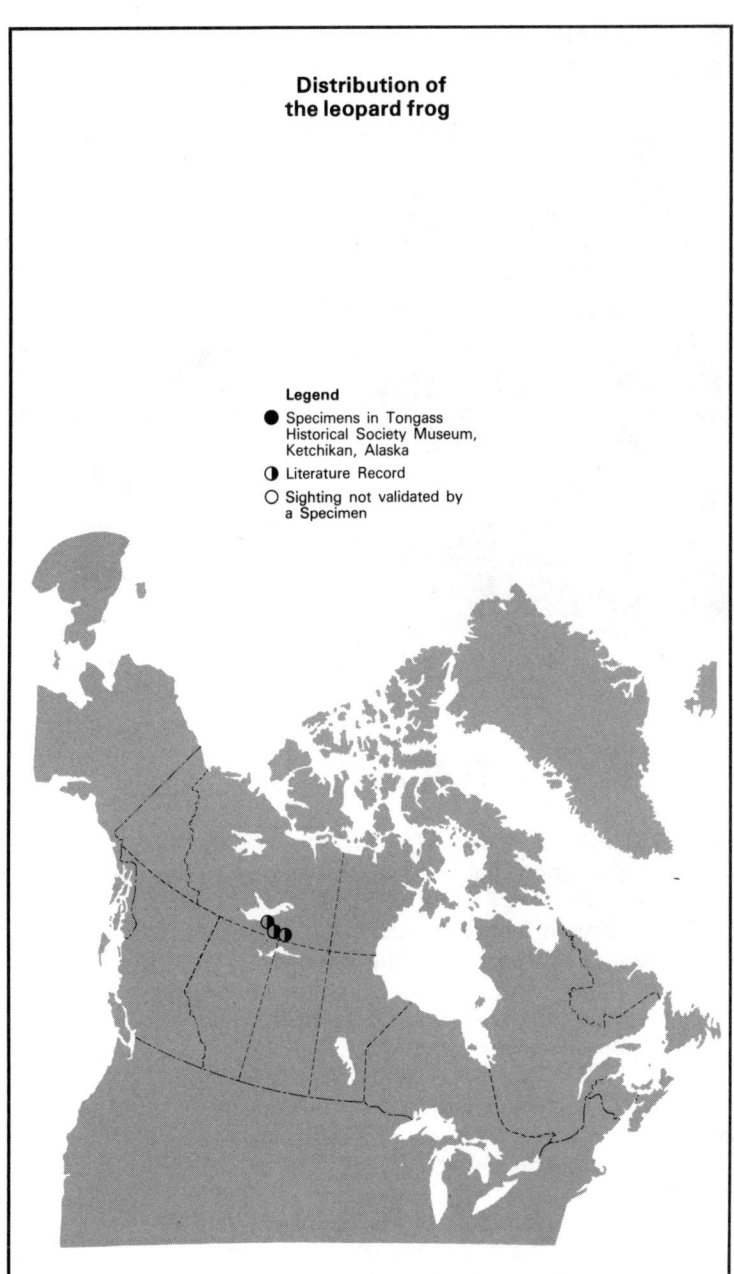

GARTER SNAKE
Thamnophis sirtalis

Thamnophis means a snake found in shrubs and *sirtalis* means "like a garter" (referring to the three dorsal stripes).

DISTINGUISHING CHARACTERS
Three prominent light stripes the length of the body.
DESCRIPTION
A dark brown (almost black) snake with three yellow stripes the length of the body. The intensity of the stripes varies considerably, from brilliant yellow to almost completely lacking. Red blotches often present between stripes. To 3½ feet (approximately 1 meter).
DISTRIBUTION IN NORTHWEST TERRITORIES
Fort Smith area of Northwest Territories.
HABITAT
Open fields near water.
REMARKS
Occasionally may bite, but is harmless. When first captured may expel feces and foul-smelling fluid from anal scent glands. Feeds on insects and amphibians. Gives birth to living young.

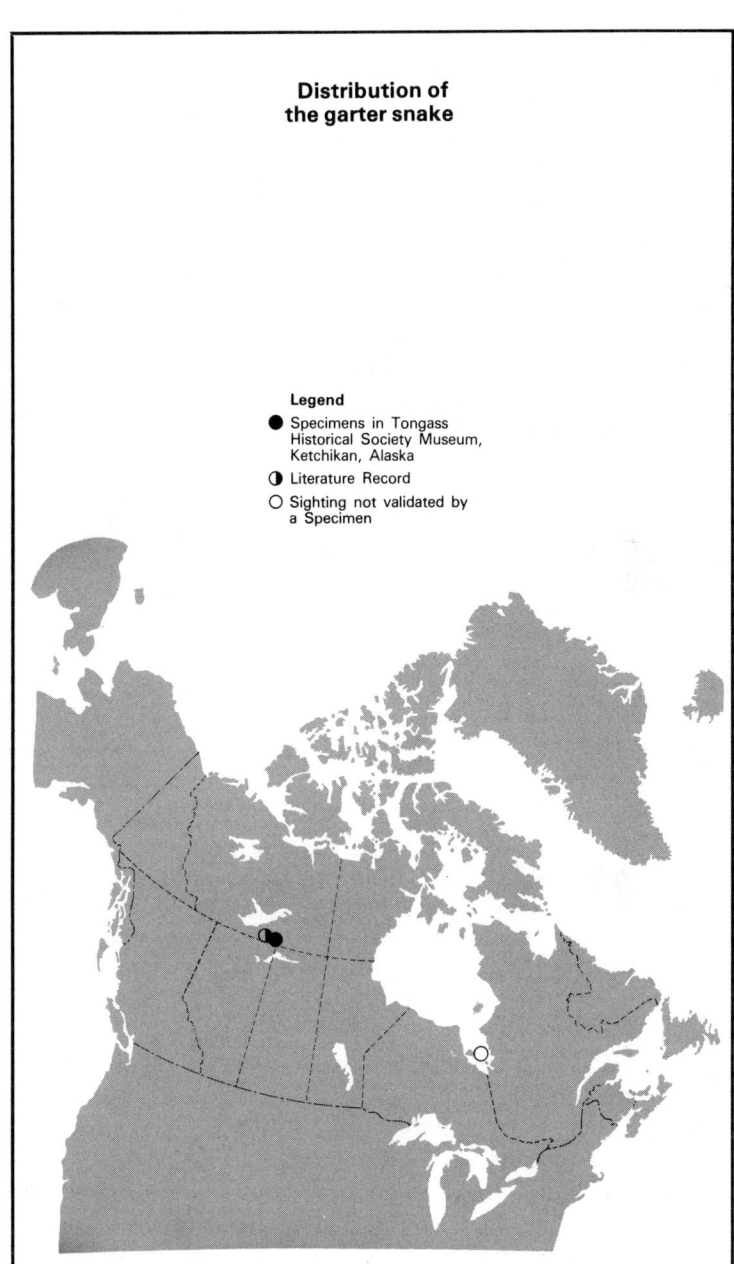

OTHER SPECIES THAT MAY BE PRESENT IN THE YUKON AND NORTHWEST TERRITORIES

At present the only amphibian known to live in the Yukon is the wood frog. But as very little herpetological work has been done in the territory, additional species may be discovered. The most likely ones are the chorus frog and garter snake, entering the Yukon via northeastern British Columbia, and the boreal toad, spotted frog and long-toed salamander in the mountains of extreme southwestern Yukon.

The Northwest Territories might also yield additional species. The long-toed salamander and the wandering garter snake, *Thamnophis elegans*, have been collected on the banks of the Peace River at the British Columbia/Alberta border. A thousand miles downriver at Fort Smith, where that river system flows into the Northwest Territories, several knowledgeable persons have seen dull brown "cliff snakes" — possibly *Thamnophis elegans* — in addition to the vividly marked black, yellow and red *Thamnophis sirtalis* on the banks of the river there. The wandering garter snakes captured on the Peace River at the British Columbia/Alberta border are large, robust, uniformly slate brown, some with and some without faint darker stripes, differing markedly from the common garter snake found in that area. The two species are easily distinguished.

As more extensive field work on the islands in James Bay is initiated, additional amphibians may be recorded there. The spring peeper, *Hyla crucifer,* has been recorded as far north as Attawapiskat, Ontario, which lies due west of Akimiski Island. The leopard frog, *Rana pipiens,* is found on the adjacent mainland much farther north of the larger islands. The mink frog, *Rana septentrionalis,* a large aquatic northern frog which has been discovered in extreme northern Quebec, requires large permanent bodies of water with abundant growth of water lilies. Such bodies of water exist in abundance on Charlton and Akimiski Islands.

Reptiles likely to be recorded on the islands in James Bay include the eastern form of the garter snake, *Thamnophis sirtalis.* Additional eastern North American amphibians that approach the James Bay region include the blue-spotted salamander, *Ambystoma laterale,* and the red-backed salamander, *Phethodon cinerus.*

WHAT YOU CAN DO

Over the past 6 years, the author has traveled over 50,000 miles throughout Alaska and the Canadian territories studying amphibians and reptiles. The distances traveled would be quite impressive if one were involved with the herpetology of Rhode Island, which has an area of only 1,214 square miles; however, Alaska alone has 586,400 square miles and the Yukon and Northwest Territories combined possess an additional 1,511,979 square miles! True, these areas do not possess the diverse herpetofauna that miniscule Rhode Island is fortunate to have, but it remains quite obvious that there is much to be discovered about the amphibians and reptiles of the North.

Interested residents throughout Alaska and the Canadian territories are encouraged to make observations "in their own backyard" and keep a detailed notebook. The importance of maintaining such a notebook of field observations cannot be overemphasized. Much significant information can be accumulated by religiously jotting down observations gathered over a period of time. In addition to offering meaningful outdoor activity, significant facts of considerable scientific value might be accumulated. Throughout most of their respective ranges, the majority of amphibians and reptiles overproduce, so *limited* collecting has little negative effects on herpetological conservation. However, northern animals at the peripheral margins of their ranges (long-toed and northwestern salamanders, garter snakes) are vulnerable to overexploitation in the form of zealous collectors. Yet our knowledge of northern herpetology depends on the orderly assemblage of representative specimens deposited in a recognized public museum where they can be studied by interested individuals. Instead of just plunging forth into the bush and plunking every frog encountered into a collecting jar, the prospective collector is urged to be discriminating. If you observe an amphibian or reptile in Alaska or the Canadian territories and wish to share your observation with the author, simply write the Tongass Historical Society Museum, Post Office Box 674, Ketchikan, Alaska 99901, sending the following information: what the animal looked like (include a simple sketch based on drawings in this book), color, where the animal was found, and the date of finding. If, after examining the information on your post card, the museum desires your specimen, you will be notified as to preserving and shipping instructions.

The keeping of native amphibians and reptiles as pets for *extended* periods of time is to be discouraged. Finding suitable live food for a starving frog, that normally would be hibernating, in January in Fairbanks can be somewhat of a problem. However, confining a few individuals in a suitable container for short periods of time for close observation is justifiable, often yielding significant observations. Adult amphibians can be kept in aquariums and require nothing more than food, moisture, moderate temperatures, and shelter from direct sunlight. Frogs, toads and salamanders eat worms and insects. Reptiles require warm, dry, escapeproof containers. A small water dish should be in the cage at all times and insects, worms and small amphibians offered as food. Much useful and fascinating information can be gleaned by placing amphibian egg masses in containers of pond water and observing and recording rates of development prior to hatching and subsequent tadpole development and behavior. Tadpoles require abundant amounts of food (algae and detritus) and salamander larvae require minute living crustaceans and insect larvae. Once metamorphosis is completed, the young adults and any other temporary captives should be released *where they were captured,* and long before the first severe freeze of autumn.

APPENDIX: HERPETOLOGICAL COLLECTIONS
TONGASS HISTORICAL SOCIETY MUSEUM, KETCHIKAN, ALASKA

001 *Rana sylvatica,* Stagg River, Northwest Territories, Canada
002 *Rana sylvatica,* Louise Falls, Northwest Territories, Canada
003 *Rana sylvatica,* Fort Providence, Northwest Territories, Canada
004 *Thamnophis sirtalis,* Salt River, Northwest Territories, Canada
005 *Bufo americanus copei,* Goose Bay, Labrador, Canada
006 *Rana sylvatica,* Mile 941, Alaska Highway, Yukon, Canada
007 *Rana sylvatica,* Mile 941, Alaska Highway, Yukon, Canada
008 *Rana sylvatica,* Soldotna, Alaska
009 *Taricha granulosa,* Shelter Island, Alaska
010 *Bufo boreas,* Dredge Lake, Juneau, Alaska
011 *Bufo boreas,* Dredge Lake, Juneau, Alaska
012 *Bufo boreas,* Dredge Lake, Juneau, Alaska
013 *Bufo boreas,* Skagway, Alaska
014 *Bufo boreas,* Mendenhall Glacier, Alaska
015 *Bufo boreas,* Mendenhall Glacier, Alaska
016 *Bufo boreas,* Mendenhall Glacier, Alaska
017 *Rana pretiosa,* Twin Lakes (Stikine River), Alaska
018 *Bufo boreas,* Annette Island, Alaska
019 *Ambystoma macrodactylum,* Twin Lakes (Stikine River), Alaska
020 *Taricha granulosa,* Ward Lake, Ketchikan, Alaska
021 *Bufo boreas,* Ward Lake, Ketchikan, Alaska
022 *Taricha granulosa,* Annette Island, Alaska
023 *Taricha granulosa,* Annette Bay, Alaska
024 *Rana sylvatica,* Twin Lakes (Stikine River), Alaska
025 *Bufo boreas,* Twin Lakes (Stikine River), Alaska
026 *Ambystoma macrodactylum,* Twin Lakes (Stikine River), Alaska
027 *Bufo boreas,* Twin Lakes (Stikine River), Alaska
028 *Rana sylvatica,* Hot Springs (Stikine River), Alaska
029 *Taricha granulosa,* Wrangell Reservoir, Alaska
030 *Taricha granulosa,* Annette Bay, Alaska
031 *Bufo boreas,* Annette Bay, Alaska
032 *Bufo boreas,* Twin Lakes (Stikine River), Alaska
033 *Taricha granulosa,* Wrangell Reservoir, Alaska
034 *Rana pretiosa,* Twin Lakes (Stikine River), Alaska
035 *Rana sylvatica,* Hot Springs (Stikine River), Alaska
036 *Ambystoma macrodactylum,* Twin Lakes (Stikine River), Alaska
037 *Rana sylvatica,* Anchorage, Alaska
038 *Rana sylvatica,* Petersburg, Alaska

039 *Rana sylvatica,* Anchorage, Alaska
040 *Bufo boreas,* Yakutat, Alaska
041 *Rana sylvatica,* Fort Yukon, Alaska
042 *Rana pretiosa,* Petersburg, Alaska
043 *Rana sylvatica,* College, Alaska
044 *Rana sylvatica,* Anchorage, Alaska
045 *Rana sylvatica,* Fairbanks, Alaska
046 *Rana sylvatica,* Anchorage, Alaska
047 *Rana sylvatica,* Livengood, Alaska
048 *Pseudacris triseriata,* Fort St. John, British Columbia, Canada
049 *Bufo americanus,* Moosonee (James Bay), Ontario, Canada
050 *Rana pipiens,* Moosonee (James Bay), Ontario, Canada
051 *Pseudacris triseriata,* Moosonee (James Bay), Ontario, Canada
052 *Rana sylvatica,* Moosonee (James Bay), Ontario, Canada
053 *Bufo boreas,* Fort St. John, British Columbia, Canada
054 *Pseudacris triseriata,* Ministik Lake, Alberta, Canada
055 *Rana pipiens,* Grand Forks, Alberta, Canada
056 *Bufo hemiophrys,* Red Deer River, Alberta, Canada
057 *Rana pipiens,* Milk River, Alberta, Canada
058 *Bufo hemiophrys,* Buffalo Lake, Alberta, Canada
059 *Rana pipiens,* Milk River, Alberta, Canada
060 *Rana sylvatica,* Hay River, Northwest Territories, Canada
061 *Rana sylvatica,* Fort St. John, British Columbia, Canada
062 *Thamnophis elegans* (DOR), Fort St. John, British Columbia, Canada
063 *Thamnophis sirtalis* (DOR), Fort St. John, British Columbia, Canada
064 *Ambystoma gracile,* Kitimat, British Columbia, Canada
065 *Thamnophis sirtalis,* Mile 18, Alaska Highway, British Columbia, Canada
066 *Ambystoma gracile,* Kitimat, British Columbia, Canada
067 *Ambystoma gracile,* Kitimat, British Columbia, Canada
068 *Thamnophis sirtalis* (skin), Mile 18, Alaska Highway, British Columbia, Canada
069 *Bufo boreas,* Mary Island, Alaska
070 *Rana sylvatica,* Mile 58, Alaska Highway, British Columbia, Canada
071 *Bufo boreas,* Moberly Lake, British Columbia, Canada
072 *Bufo boreas,* Moberly Lake, British Columbia, Canada
073 *Rana sylvatica,* Peace River at Taylor, British Columbia, Canada
074 *Thamnophis elegans* (DOR), Hudson's Hope, British Columbia, Canada
075 *Thamnophis sirtalis* (DOR), Hudson's Hope, British Columbia, Canada
076 *Thamnophis sirtalis* (DOR), Hudson's Hope, British Columbia, Canada
077 *Bufo boreas,* Taylor, British Columbia, Canada
078 *Bufo boreas,* Taylor, British Columbia, Canada
079 *Bufo boreas,* Taylor, British Columbia, Canada
080 *Ambystoma macrodactylum,* Peace River at Taylor, British Columbia, Canada
081 *Ambystoma macrodactylum,* Peace River at Taylor, British Columbia, Canada
082 *Ambystoma gracile,* Kitimat, British Columbia, Canada
083 *Ambystoma gracile,* Kitimat, British Columbia, Canada
084 *Thamnophis elegans,* Taylor, British Columbia, Canada
085 *Thamnophis elegans,* Taylor, British Columbia, Canada
086 *Bufo boreas,* Pelican, Alaska

DOR = Dead on the road.

READING LIST

Ashton, R.E., Jr.; Gutman, S.I.; and Buckley, P. 1973. Notes on the distribution, coloration, and breeding of the Hudson Bay toad, *Bufo Americanus copei* (Yarrow and Henshaw). *Journal of Herpetology* 7:17-20.

Beals, C.S. 1968. *Science, history and Hudson Bay.* 2 vols. Ottawa: Dept. of Energy, Mines, and Resources.

Bean, T.H. 1882. *Notes on a collection of fishes made in 1882-1883 in Alaska and British Columbia with a description of a new genus and species, Prionistius macellus.* Proceedings of the U.S. National Museum 6:353-361.

Bellis, E.D. 1965. Home range and movements of the wood frog in a northern bog. *Ecology* 46:90-98.

Bellis, Edward David. 1957. *An ecological study of the frog Rana sylvatica Le Conte.* Minneapolis: University of Minnesota.

Bishop, Sherman. 1947. *Handbook of salamanders.* Ithaca, New York: Comstock Publishing Co.

Blair, W.F. 1972. *Evolution in the genus Bufo.* Austin: University of Texas Press.

Bleakney, J. Sherman. 1958. *A zoogeographical study of the amphibians and reptiles of eastern Canada.* Ottawa: National Museum of Canada.

— — —. 1959. Postglacial dispersal of the western chorus frog in eastern Canada. *Canadian Field Naturalist* 73: 197-205.

Bodsworth, Fred. 1970. The Pacific Coast. *The illustrated natural history of Canada.* Toronto: Natural Science of Canada.

Braithwaite, Max. 1970. The western plains. *The illustrated natural history of Canada.* Toronto: Natural Science of Canada.

Brame, Arden. 1967. A list of the world's recent and fossil salamanders. *Journal of the Southwestern Herpetology Society* 2:1-26.

Breckenridge, W.J. 1944. *Reptiles and amphibians of Minnesota.* Minneapolis: University of Minnesota Press.

Browder, L.W.; Underhill, J.C.; Merrell, D.J. 1966. Mid-dorsal stripe in the wood frog. *Journal of Heredity* 57:65-67.

Caras, Roger. 1974. *Venomous animals of the world.* Englewood Cliffs: Prentice Hall.

Carl, G. Clifford. 1959. *The amphibians of British Columbia.* Victoria: British Columbia Provincial Museum.

———. 1960. *The reptiles of British Columbia.* Victoria: British Columbia Provincial Museum.

Carr, Archie. 1967. *So excellent a fishe: A natural history of sea turtles.* New York: Doubleday & Co., Anchor Press.

Coates, Donald. 1951. Mapping the North. *Canadian Geographical Journal* 43.

Colbert, E.H. 1973. *Wandering lands and animals.* New York: E.P. Dutton & Co.

Conant, Roger. 1958. *A field guide to the reptiles and amphibians.* Boston: Houghton Mifflin Co.

Cook, F.R. 1964. A northern range extension for *Bufo americanus* with notes on *B. americanus* and *Rana sylvatica. Canadian Field Naturalist* 78:65-66.

———. 1966. *Amphibians and reptiles of Saskatchewan.* Regina: Saskatchewan Museum of Natural History.

———. 1967. An analysis of the herpetofauna of Prince Edward Island. *Bulletin 212.* Ottawa: National Museum of Canada.

———. 1970. Rare or endangered Canadian amphibians and reptiles. *Canadian Field Naturalist* 84:9-16.

Cope, E.D. 1889. The *Batrachia* of North America. *Bulletin of the U.S. National Museum* 34:1-525.

Cott, H.B. 1940. *Adaptive coloration in animals.* London: Methuen & Co.

Darlington, P.J. 1957. *Zoogeography.* New York: John Wiley & Sons.

Dickerson, M.C. 1969. *The frog book.* New York: Dover Publications.

Dunn, E.R. 1926. *The salamanders of the family Plethodontidae.* Northampton, Massachusetts: Smith College.

———. 1944. Notes on the salamanders of the *Ambystoma gracile* group. *Copeia,* 1944, no. 3, pp. 129-130.

Edwards, R. 1970. The mountain barrier. *The illustrated natural history of Canada.* Toronto: Natural Science of Canada.

Ferguson, B.E. 1956. The distribution of *Rana sylvatica cantabrigenus baird* in western Canada and Alaska. *Herpetologica* 12 (part 1): 132.

Fishbeck, D.W., and Underhill, J.C. 1971. Distribution of stripe polymorphism in wood frogs, *Rana sylvatica Le Conte,* from Minnesota. *Copeia,* 1971, no. 2, pp. 253-259.

Froom, Barbara. 1972. *The snakes of Canada.* Toronto: McClelland and Stewart.

Garfield, V.E., and Forrest, L.A. 1969. *The wolf and the raven.* Seattle: University of Washington Press.

Godfrey, W. Earl. 1951. Notes on the birds of southern Yukon Territory. *Bulletin 123.* Ottawa: National Museum of Canada.

Gosner, K.I. 1960. A simplified table for staging anuran embryos and larvae with notes of identification. *Herpetologica* 16:181-190.

Hadley, Raymond S. 1960. *The effects of season and temperature on certain aspects of the physiology of the Alaskan wood frog Rana sylvatica.* Fairbanks: University of Alaska.

Hansen, Henry. 1967. *Arctic biology.* Corvallis: Oregon State University Press.

Herreid, C.F., and Kenney, S. 1967. Temperature and development of the wood frog, *Rana sylvatica,* in Alaska. *Ecology* 48:579-590.

Hilderbrans, H. 1949. Notes on *Rana sylvatica* in the Labrador Peninsula. *Copeia,* 1949, no. 3, pp. 168-172.

Hock, R.J. 1957. Alaska zoogeography and Alaskan amphibia. *Proceedings of the Alaska Science Conference 1953.* Anchorage: published privately. Available at University of Alaska Library, Fairbanks.

Hodge, Robert P. 1972. *Neklinyuk, the northern frog.* Tacoma: Erco Publishing Co.

— — —. 1973. *Ambystoma macrodactylum* discovered in Alaska. *Hiss News Journal* 1:623.

Hopkins, David. 1967. *The Bering land bridge.* Stanford: Stanford University Press.

Hosie, R.C. 1969. *Native trees of Canada.* Ottawa: Canadian Foresty Service.

Howe, R.H. 1899. North American wood frogs. *Proceedings of the Boston Society of Natural History* 28:369-374.

Hubbs, C. 1958. *Zoogeography.* Washington, D.C.: American Association for the Advancement of Science.

Hulten, Eric. 1968. *Flora of Alaska.* Stanford: Stanford University Press.

Indian children of British Columbia. 1973. *Tales from the longhouse.* Sidney, British Columbia: Gray's Publishing.

Johansen, K. 1962. Observation on the wood frog, *Rana sylvatica,* in Alaska. *Ecology* 43:146-147.

Karlstrom, E.I. 1966. The northwestern toad, *Bufo boreas borcus,* in central Alaska: A study of the ectotherm at the northern limit of its species range. In *Science in Alaska.* Abstract from *Proceedings of the 17th Alaskan Science Conference.*

Karlstrom, N.V. 1961. The glacial history of Alaska, its bearing on paleoclimatic theory. *Annals of the New York Academy of Sciences* 95:290-340.

Kellogg, P.P., and Allen, A.A. 1948. Voices of the night: The calls of 34 frogs and toads of the U.S. and Canada. 33 ⅓ rpm phonograph record. *Sounds of Nature.* Boston: Houghton Mifflin Co.

Kessel, Brian. 1965. Breeding dates of *Rana sylvatica* at College, Alaska. *Ecology* 46:206-208.

Kinney, Stephen Baldwin. 1966. *Developmental adaptations and breeding behavior of the Alaskan wood frog, Rana sylvatica.* Fairbanks: University of Alaska.

Kirton, Michael P. 1974. *Fall movements and hibernation of the wood frog, Rana sylvatica, in Interior Alaska.* Fairbanks: University of Alaska.

Knauth, Percy. 1972. *Northwoods.* New York: Time-Life Books.

Little, E.L., and Viereck, L.A. 1972. *Alaska trees and shrubs.* Washington, D.C.: Forest Service, U.S. Dept. of Agriculture.

Logier, E.B.S., and Toner, G.C. 1961. Check list of the amphibians and reptiles of Canada and Alaska. Toronto: Royal Ontario Museum.

Loveridge, Arthur. 1946. *Reptiles of the Pacific world.* New York: Macmillan Co.

Lui, Oh'eng-Chao. 1950. *Amphibians of western China.* Chicago: Chicago Natural History Museum.

Martof, B.S. 1970. Rana sylvatica. *Catalogue of American amphibians and reptiles* 86:1.86.4.

Martof, B.S., and Humphries, R.L. 1950. Geographic variation in the wood frog, *Rana sylvatica. American Midland Naturalist* 61:350-389.

May, Charles Paul. 1964. *Animals of the Far North.* New York: Abelard-Schuman.

McPhail, J.D., and Lindsey, C.C. 1970. *Fresh water fishes of northwestern Canada and Alaska.* Ottawa: Fisheries Research Board of Canada.

Meteorological Branch, Dept. of Transport. 1962. *The climate of Canada.* Ottawa: Information Canada.

Miller, J.D. 1976. An extension of the range of the northern long-toed salamander, *Ambystoma macrodactylum columbianum,* in Alaska. *Canadian Field Naturalist* 90:81-82.

Mills, R.C. 1948. A check list of the reptiles and amphibians of Canada. *Herpetologica* 4 (2nd supplement):1-15.

Moon, Barbara. 1970. The Canadian Shield. *The illustrated natural history of Canada.* Toronto: Natural Science of Canada.

Moore, J.A. 1939. Temperature tolerance and rates of development in eggs of amphibia. *Ecology* 20:459-478.

———. 1951. Hybridization and embryonic temperature adaptation studies of *Rana temporaria* and *Rana sylvatica. Proceedings of the National Academy of Sciences* 37:862-866.

Neil, Wilfred. 1969. *The geography of life.* New York: Columbia University Press.

Nikol'skii, A.M. 1951. *Fauna of Russia and adjacent countries:* Amphibians. Washington, D.C.: National Science Foundation.

Noble, G. Kingsley. 1954. *The biology of the amphibia.* 1931. Reprint. New York: Dover Publications.

Okada, Yaldriro. 1966. *Fauna Japonica (anura).* Tokyo: Tokai University Tokyo Electrical Engineering College Press.

Oliver, James. 1955. The natural history of North American reptiles and amphibians. New York: D. Van Nostrand Co.

Patch, Clyde. 1939. Northern records of the wood frog. *Copeia,* 1939, no. 4, p. 235.

Pickwell, Gayle. 1972. *Amphibians and reptiles of the Pacific states.* New York: Dover Publications.

Porter, Kenneth R. 1972. *Herpetology.* Philadelphia: W.B. Saunders Co.

Preble, F.A. 1902. A biological investigation of the Hudson Bay region. *North American Fauna* 22:1-140.

Pritchard, P.C.H. 1971. *The leatherback or leathery turtle, Dermochelys coriacea.* Morges: The International Union for Conservation of Nature and Natural Resources.

Sage, Bryan. 1973. *Alaska and its wildlife.* New York: Viking Press.

Schmidt, Karl P. 1938. A geographic variation gradient in frogs. *Zoological Series of the Field Museum of Natural History* 20:377-382.

Schueler, F.W. 1973. Frogs of the Ontario coast of Hudson Bay and James Bay. *Canadian Field Naturalist* 87:409-418.

Slevin, J.R. 1928. *The amphibians of western North America.* San Francisco: California Academy of Sciences.

Smith, Malcolm. 1951. *The British amphibians and reptiles.* London: William Collins Sons.

Stebbins, R. 1954. *Amphibians and reptiles of western North America.* New York: McGraw Hill Book Co.

―――. 1966. *A field guide to western reptiles and amphibians.* Boston: Houghton Mifflin Co.

Steward, J.W. 1970. The tailed amphibians of Europe. New York: Taplinger Publishing Co.

Stonehouse, Bernard. 1971. *Animals of the arctic: Ecology of the Far North.* New York: Holt, Rinehart & Winston.

Swarth, H.S. 1936. Origins of the fauna of the Sitkan district, Alaska. *Proceedings of the California Academy of Sciences* 23:59-78.

Terent'ev, P.V. 1961. *Herpetology*. Translated from the Russian by the Israel Program for Scientific Translations, Jerusalem, 1965. Springfield, Virginia: U.S. Dept. of Commerce Clearinghouse for Federal Scientific and Technical Information.

Wake, David. 1966. Comparative osteology and evolution of the lungless salamanders family *Plethodontidae. Memoirs of the Southern California Academy of Sciences* 4.

Wherry, J.H. 1969. *The totem pole Indians.* New York: Funk and Wagnalls.

Wright, A.H., and Wright, A.A. 1949. *Handbook of frogs and toads.* Ithaca, New York: Comstock Publishing Co.

— — —. 1957. *Handbook of snakes.* 2 vols. Ithaca, New York: Comstock Publishing Associates.

Wynne-Edwards, V.C. 1952. *Freshwater vertebrates of the arctic and subarctic.* Ottawa: Fisheries Research Board of Canada.